D0501333

11/6/80

LANDSCAPE PLANTS OF THE SOUTHEAST

LANDSCAPE PLANTS OF THE SOUTHEAST

R. GORDON HALFACRE
AND
ANNE R. SHAWCROFT

SPARKS PRESS
Post Office Box 26747
Raleigh, North Carolina 27611

ISBN 0-916822-10-9
Library of Congress Catalog Card Number: 79-8 8976

To Angela and Robert

CONTENTS

ACKNOWLEDGMENTS

Many people have contributed to the material in *Landscape Plants of the Southeast* and we gratefully acknowledge their support. Special thanks are extended to John H. Harris and to Dr. Clive W. Donoho, Jr., for their inspiration and encouragement. For assistance in the organization and preparation of the manuscript, appreciation is expressed to Robert E. Marvin, Landscape Architect, Walterboro, South Carolina; Richard C. Bell, Landscape Architect, Raleigh, North Carolina; Howard M. Singletary, and Dr. Roy A. Larson, Horticultural Science, North Carolina State University; Dr. J. C. Wells, Plant Pathology, North Carolina State University; Dr. Robert L. Robertson, Entomology, North Carolina State University; Richard R. Wilkinson, Landscape Architecture, North Carolina State University; Jim Kellison, Artist, Raleigh, North Carolina; Charles O. Bell, Grounds Superintendent, University of North Carolina at Greensboro; Ellis Jourdain Moore, John P. Fulmer, Dr. David Bradshaw and Mary Taylor, Horticulture Department, Clemson University; Ronald Copeland, Apex Nursery, Apex, North Carolina; Helen Weaver, Artist, Clemson, South Carolina; Dr. Henry Orr, Horticulture Department, Auburn University; Dr. Alfred E. Einert, Landscape Architect, Horticulture Department, University of Arkansas and to Carolyn Halfacre appreciation is expressed for assistance with the text.

R.G.H.
A.R.S.

INTRODUCTION

Landscape Plants of the Southeast presents information on 600 plants most useful for landscaping purposes in the Southeast. It brings together all facts on plant materials needed to create interesting and successful landscape designs.

In this book plants are grouped by type and height for landscape use. Usually shrubs and trees are arranged according to plant families. Since this is of little value to landscape gardeners, another method has been employed. All plants are grouped into 7 easily distinguished main categories — ground covers, vines, shrubs 1-4 feet high, shrubs 4-6 feet high, shrubs 6-12 feet high, small trees, and large trees.

The Latin and common names of plants conform to the International Code for the Nomenclature of Cultivated Plants which went into effect in January 1959. Clonal or English varietal names are given in single quotation marks; horticultural varieties are in italics.

The scientific name of a plant is made up of 2 words, for example, *Ajuga reptans*. The first word represents the genus or group to which the plant belongs and is always written with a capital letter. The second word indicates the species or kind and is rarely capitalized. The meanings of the genus and species are given to aid in understanding the scientific terms.

The following illustration will relate the association of species, genus, and family. In this book there are 5 kinds or species of roses, Memorial Rose, Rugose Rose, Japanese Rose, Climbing Rose, and Banks Rose. They all belong to the group or genus *Rosa* and are known respectively as *Rosa wichuraiana*, *Rosa rugosa*, *Rosa multiflora*, *Rosa hybrida*, and *Rosa banksiae*. Somewhat closely related to roses are strawberry, spirea, pyracantha, photinia, hawthorn, cotoneaster, and quince. These different genera (plural of genus) together with several others form a larger relationship that is known as the rose family, or Rosaceae. The ending — aceae, which is generally used to denote a family, is the feminine plural of the Latin suffix—aceus, meaning like or related to.

Information on the individual species is presented uniformly for ease in comparison of characteristics. Following is an explanation of this descriptive information.

Zones. The zone numbers listed for each plant refer to the map of average minimum temperatures for zones 6, 7, and 8 on page xvi. These zones indicate areas of the Southeast where the plant grows well without protection.

Size. Size indicates the height and spread of mature plants. The extremes are given, as 4-6 feet, which means that somewhere between these figures is the average height of growth attained within a reasonable time under average cultural conditions. Immature plants will be below that average, but many plants under optimum conditions will exceed heights shown in this book. The spread indicated is the average width of the plant when it is not affected by crowding.

Size in planting design is essential. Plants should be in proportion with the background; a small garden may be overpowered by a large tree. With a limited garden area and a small house, emphasis should be on low and medium sized shrubs and trees. However, small shrubs against a massive building will usually seem lost and completely out of scale.

Form. There is great variation of form or shape in plants. Form may be called the architecture of plants. Line patterns of branches vary from upright to spreading, arching, or horizontal.

Select plants that will achieve the desired visual effect. Vertical branching leads the line of view upward; horizontal branching ties the view to ground forms. Weeping forms in plants complement rolling terrain and steep banks. Tall and upright plant forms are useful emphasis points in the repetition and regularity of formal gardens. Tight, neatly rounded plants such as boxwood are used in formal design. Informal design usually calls for loose-growing plants, such as azalea and waxmyrtle.

Density of habit of growth must be considered in achieving balance in design. Plants such as boxwood and yew are heavy and compact in form, while waxmyrtle and azalea are light and open. Compact hollies balance the loose form of taller dogwoods; light white pines balance heavy pyracanthas. Many deciduous trees and shrubs have interesting line patterns when they are dormant. Crape-myrtle and dogwood branches are especially attractive in winter.

Texture. Texture is the relationship of size, surface, appearance, and general distribution of branches, twigs, and foliage to the complete plant. Plants are classified as either fine, medium, or coarse in texture. Examples are fine — weeping willow, cotoneaster, and spirea; medium — azalea, sasanqua, and cleyera; and coarse — Southern magnolia, loquat, and aucuba.

As a general rule, fine-textured plants enrich architecture having smooth surfaces and fine lines; coarse textured plants complement large spaces and coarse building materials.

Variety should be introduced but handled carefully to avoid confusion. Change in size, texture, form, or color may be used to bring emphasis to a certain area. Maintain unity in at least two of the basic qualities, such as size and foliage color, and vary the third. For example, to emphasize a particular feature, use varying leaf textures while maintaining similar color and form throughout the planting.

Color. Far too much dependence upon flower color for interest in garden design is evident. Color is seasonal but good foliage and lines are relatively permanent. Use color with restraint and as an accent. Color is provided by leaves, berries, and bark as well as flowers. Care should be taken to maintain harmony between plant colors and background elements.

Culture. Often plants are selected for landscape design without considering the cultural aspects such as sun or shade exposure, soil, moisture, pruning, pest problems, and growth rate. When plants are placed in an unsuitable environment, constant maintenance problems will occur.

The terms sun, part shade, or shade refer to the quantity of light in which a plant grows best. Some plants cannot endure sun, while others require full sun for best display.

Soil requirements for plants vary widely. For best growth and development, plant only in the soil conditions recommended. The term "drainage" indicates the freedom of moisture movement downward through the soil and not the slope of the soil surface. The following conditions affect soil drainage. Poor drainage is found in very heavy clay; medium drainage is found in good garden soil consisting of a desirable combination of sand or gravel, clay, and organic matter; good drainage is found in gravelly soil or very sandy loam with no obstructing formations to impede water movement. Fertility of the soil is judged by the amounts of nitrogen, phosphate, and potassium present. Organic matter and trace minerals are also factors in soil fertility. With few exceptions, most landscape plants require at least medium soil fertility for best growth.

Plants are classified as either low, medium, or high in moisture requirements. For example, santolina and yucca thrive in low moisture conditions, but photinia and spirea prefer medium moisture. Weeping willow and waxmyrtle require high moisture conditions for best results.

Pruning for most plant materials involves thinning and heading back to maintain desired sizes. For plants which require special practices, specific recommendations have been made.

Most plants are susceptible to some diseases or insects. Select plants for landscape use that are relatively free of pest problems or be prepared to follow a spray schedule. Plants that are grown out of their habitat are more subject to pest problems than those growing in their native environment.

Plants have characteristic rates of growth. Although growth rate is of minor importance, it is a factor to consider in choosing a plant for a specific purpose. Sometimes rapidly growing plants are needed to fill a space quickly or to protect finer but slower-growing plants. However, many rapidly growing plants are brittle and can be used only temporarily or in protected locations.

Landscape Notes. In this section are suggestions and characteristics of plants for landscape use. Many of the comments are personal observations from experience in planting design.

Plant materials should be used to serve definite functions or solve specific problems. If a plant does not do this, it should be left out of the design. Shrubs should not be scattered over the yard to try to show off each plant. This detracts from the overall design and also creates a mowing problem. Remember, the object is to complement the house and not compete with it for interest. Some of the functions of plant materials are accent, softening, separation or screening, shade, framing, and background.

Accent shrub plantings may be used to attract or focus attention on the main entrance of the house, and both shrubs and trees may be used for this purpose in the family living area. Normally these are the only two areas where accent plantings should be used. A good design can be destroyed by using upright evergreens or other accent plants along the front of the house or on corners.

As an accent, a plant must possess one or more distinctive characteristics. It must be outstanding in form, texture, size, color, or have a combination of these qualities. Often an accent plant is most effective when used with other plants that emphasize its characteristics. For example, a plant with coarse texture used with plants having fine texture would make a good combination. The same principle works with form, color, or size.

Corners, sharp angles, exposed high foundations, and massive walls should be visually softened by plantings. Plants selected should not attract attention or dominate. Consider these questions. If a corner of a house is to be softened, how large will the plants need to grow? Will the choices blend with other nearby plants? Plants should be massed at the corners of a building; a single plant is rarely effective. Use a small group of shrubs spaced so that they will grow together upon reaching maturity. Medium and small shrubs work well for one-story houses. Two-story houses may require large or medium shrub plantings; the best are irregular and inconspicuous in form but not unusual in foliage, color, and texture.

Shrubs are often used in borders to separate areas, to screen unpleasant views, to serve as wind barriers, and to give privacy or enclosure. In a border or mass planting, use several shrubs of one type before changing to another species. For example, place 10 or 12 ligustrums in a group or row, then continue with 8 or 10 photinias. If further extension is needed, a third choice may be used, or continue with more ligustrums. This approach will result in unity, harmony, and a well-planned border.

The choice of shrubs to serve as screening material is nearly limitless. The best shrubs for screening are large in size, irregular or oval in form, and standard in color and texture; an ultimate height of 6-12 feet is often best. Dense, low-branching plants should be used.

Trees provide protection from undesirable winter and summer winds and screen unsightly views. For winter wind protection evergreen trees are best. Deciduous trees dense in twig and branch mass also afford excellent wind protection. Nearly all small trees grow larger than even the largest shrubs and are used most effectively where extra tall or massive screening is needed. Small trees may be used alone or combined with shrubs in screen or border planting. The variations in height provide an interesting and pleasant change.

Summer shade is an asset to both indoor and outdoor living areas. To shade a roof or wall of a one-story house, plant medium to large trees as close as 15-20 feet from the side or 12-15 feet from the corner of the building. The lower branches should be removed as the tree grows and the canopy allowed to reach over the roof. Trees may be planted for shade on lawns and patios, but do not shade vegetable gardens or flower beds.

Trees are usually located diagonally from the corners of the house for framing; the best for this purpose are medium to large in size and round or irregular in form.

Background trees located behind the house or view are important along with framing trees in providing a total setting. Background trees should be large enough to visually break the roofline of the house when viewed from the front.

Varieties. Often a plant variety can provide the designer with superior or different features. Those included are representative of the wide choice available for general use in the Southeast.

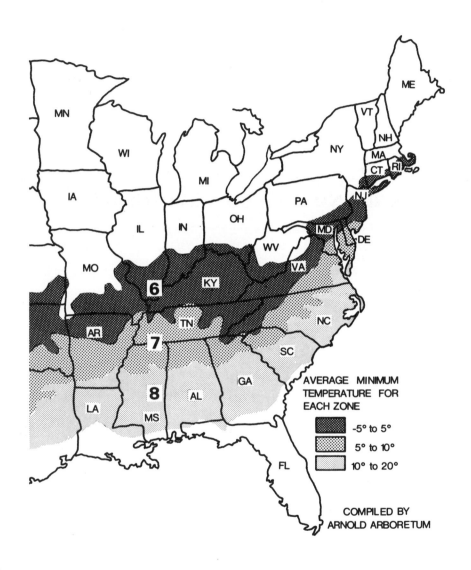

Area Zone Map for Landscape Plants.

GROUND COVERS — EVERGREEN

Ajuga (aj-oo'ga)
    Latin for not yoked,
    alluding to calyx

reptans (rep'tanz)
    creeping

BUGLEFLOWER

Family Labiatae

Zones	6, 7, 8.
Size	Height 3-5 inches; spread indeterminate.
Form	Compact, dense mat, spreading by stolons similar to strawberry. Foliage – 3-4 inches long, 1 inch wide. Flower – mid-April; small, compact pyramidal spikes.
Texture	Medium to coarse.
Color	Foliage – dark green. Flower – blue.
Culture	Part shade. Soil – well-drained; medium fertility. Moisture – high. Pruning – none. Pest Problems – aphids during rapid growth in early spring and crown rot. Growth Rate – rapid.
Landscape Notes	Excellent ground cover especially for moist locations. Good used in rock gardens and in odd corners. Space plants 6 inches apart. *A. genevensis* grows more slowly.
Varieties	*alba* – white flowers. 'Atropurpurea' – bronze foliage and blue flowers. 'Rubra' – rose flowers, more vigorous.

Aspidistra (as-pi-dis'tra)
Greek for small, round shield,
in allusion to stigma

elatior (ee-lay'ti-or)
taller

CAST-IRON PLANT

Family Liliaceae

Zones	7,8.
Size	Height 1-2 feet; spread 2-3 feet.
Form	Upright clumps of foliage; spreads slowly by rhizomes. Foliage – to 20 inches long, 2-3 inches wide. Flower – inconspicuous, bell-shaped at surface of ground.
Texture	Coarse.
Color	Foliage – blackish-green. Flower – purple.
Culture	Shade. Soil – very tolerant. Moisture – medium. Pruning – periodically remove damaged and dead foliage. Pest Problems – scale. Growth Rate – slow.
Landscape Notes	Not strictly ground cover but used in densely shaded spots for massing or accenting. Adaptable to areas with limited soil volume. Will grow under roof overhangs and in containers. Good to contrast with other textures. Grows best in Coastal Plains.
Variety	*variegata* – leaves alternately striped, green and white in varied widths. Loses stripes if planted in rich soil.

Cotoneaster (ko-to'nee-as-ter)
Greek meaning like quince

dammeri (dam'mer-eye)
named for Udo Dammer,
German botanist

BEARBERRY COTONEASTER

Family Rosaceae

Zones	6, 7, 8.
Size	Height 6-12 inches; spread to 3 feet.
Form	Prostrate with branches often rooting in moist soil. Foliage – alternate, entire, 1 inch long. Flower – early June; 1 inch diameter. Fruit – fall; berries ¼ inch, usually with 5 nutlets.
Texture	Fine.
Color	Foliage – lustrous dark green above, light green beneath. Flower – white. Fruit – bright red.
Culture	Sun to part shade. Soil – good drainage; medium to low fertility. Moisture – medium to high. Pruning – none. Pest Problems – fire blight, lacebug, red spider, and borers. Growth Rate – slow.
Landscape Notes	Effective in rock gardens or on low banks. Limit quantities in warmer locations to avoid pest and disease problems. Mulch to control weed growth between plants.
Varieties	'Lowfast' – good selection for warm areas; fairly resistant to fireblight. 'Radicans' – leaves smaller than species. 'Skogholmen' – height less than 1 foot, but stems may trail to 3 feet.

Cyrtomium (sir-to'mi-um)
   Greek for arching and
   merging

falcatum (fal-kay'tum)
   sickle-shaped

HOLLY FERN

Family Polypodiaceae

Zone	8.
Size	Height 1-2 feet; spread 2-3 feet.
Form	Upright stems forming compact clumps. Foliage – hollylike leathery pinnae, 1 2 fcct long. Sori bearing spores on underside of leaves in late summer or fall.
Texture	Coarse.
Color	Foliage – glossy dark green.
Culture	Shade or part shade. Soil – good drainage; medium fertility with high organic content. Moisture – medium. Pruning – remove dead and damaged fronds in spring. Pest Problems – none. Growth Rate – moderate.
Landscape Notes	Lends interest to small city gardens. Does not spread. Excellent as accent plant or ground cover in Coastal Plain areas.
Varieties	'Compactum' – leaves shorter than species. 'Rochefordianum' – excellent foliage. More popular than species.

Dichondra (di-kon'dra)
creeping tropical vines,
morning glory family

repens (ree'penz)
creeping

carolinensis (ka-ro-ly-nen'sis)
from Carolinas

DICHONDRA

Family Convolvulaceae

Zone	8.
Size	Height 2-3 inches; spread indeterminate.
Form	Creeping with leaves upright forming thick cover. Foliage – ½ inch diameter, rounded.
Texture	Medium to fine.
Color	Foliage – medium green.
Culture	Sun or part shade. Soil – tolerant; medium drainage; medium fertility; fertilize annually. Moisture – medium; water periodically in dry weather. Pruning – mow 3-4 times during year. Pest Problems – rust fungus, cutworms, red spider, slugs, and nematodes. Growth Rate – rapid.
Landscape Notes	Used as substitute for grass over large areas. May be sown with seeds in March to May and is sometimes called 'Leaf Lawn.' Will not stand traffic as well as grass lawn. Not hardy in mountains. Requires practically no maintenance when established.

Festuca (fes-tu'ka)
  fescue grasses

ovina (o-vi'na)
  pertaining to sheep

glauca (glaw'ka)
  glaucous

BLUE FESCUE

Family Poaceae

Zones	6, 7, 8.
Size	Height 8-12 inches; spread 8-12 inches.
Form	Singular dense tufts or clumps of grass. Foliage – narrow, 10-12 inches long. Fruit – panicles 12-14 inches long.
Texture	Fine.
Color	Foliage – silvery-blue. Fruit – light brown.
Culture	Sun to part shade. Soil – tolerant. Moisture – tolerant. Pruning – remove seed heads. Pest Problems – none. Growth Rate – medium to rapid.
Landscape Notes	Best color in full sun. Protects soil against erosion and is drought resistant. Use gravel mulch for best appearance. Excellent edging or border material but does not form solid carpet.

Fragaria (fra-gair'i-a)
　　Latin for fragrance
chiloensis (chill-o-en'sis)
　　from Chile
ananassa (a-nan'as-sa)
　　resembling pineapple
STRAWBERRY
Family Rosaceae

Zones	6, 7, 8.
Size	Height 4-12 inches; spread indeterminate.
Form	Non-climbing; medium density, propagates naturally by runners. Foliage – leaf of three dentate leaflets each 1-2 inches long. Flower – spring and summer; 1 inch in clusters. Fruit – May to June; berry ¾ -1 inch diameter.
Texture	Medium.
Color	Foliage – medium green; winter, reddish-brown. Flower – snowy white. Fruit – red.
Culture	Sun or very light shade. Soil – good drainage; medium to high fertility. Moisture – medium. Pruning – periodic thinning. Pest Problems – parasitic nematodes, mites, beetles, weevils, and other insects. Growth Rate – moderate.
Landscape Notes	Use for border planting along walks, drives, and flower beds and as garden plant. Wild strawberry also excellent for similar uses.
Varieties	'Earlibelle' – early, bright red fruit.
	'Sunrise' – early, orange-red fruit.
	'Surecrop' – midseason, red fruit; vigorous plant.

Helleborus (hell-e-bor'us)
   Christmas rose

orientalis (or-i-en-ta'lis)
   oriental, eastern

LENTEN-ROSE

Family Ranunculaceae

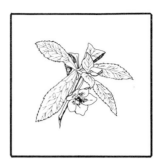

Zones	6, 7.
Size	Height 12-18 inches; spread to 12 inches.
Form	Low, erect clumps. Foliage – palmately compound, arising directly from crown, 12 inches wide. Flower – January, often remains until April; bell-shaped, 2 inches wide, 2-6 in cluster. Fruit – late spring; capsule.
Texture	Coarse.
Color	Foliage – dark green. Flower – white, fading to green or purple. Fruit – black.
Culture	Shade. Soil – tolerant; low to medium drainage; medium fertility with humus added. Moisture – medium. Pruning – none. Pest Problems – none. Growth Rate – slow until established.
Landscape Notes	Excellent cover for shaded areas; strong texture and attractive winter flowers. Space 1½ to 2 feet apart. Maximum life 10 years.
Variety	*atro-rubens* – flowers dark purple outside, greenish-purple inside.

Hypericum (hy-per'i-kum)
under or among
heather

calycinum (kal-ee-sy'num)
calyxlike

AARONSBEARD

Family Hypericaceae

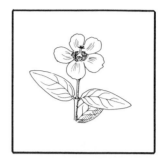

Zones	6, 7, 8.
Size	Height 8-12 inches; spread indeterminate.
Form	Procumbent, low and spreading with tufted stoloniferous growth. Foliage – opposite, 2 inches long. Flower – May and June; 3 inches wide in terminal clusters. Fruit – fall, persisting; capsules. Stems – 4-angled.
Texture	Medium.
Color	Foliage – bluish-green; fall, purplish-green. Flower – yellow with reddish anthers. Fruit – red-brown. Bark – reddish.
Culture	Sun or part shade. Soil – tolerant. Moisture – low to medium. Pruning – may discolor during cold winters and need shearing back in early spring. Pest Problems – scale. Growth Rate – rapid.
Landscape Notes	Flowering mass which completely covers the ground; useful as undershrub in woods and for rockeries; also useful in sandy soil. Good for covering large, rough areas and for erosion control. Shade limits flower production.

Iberis (eye-beer'is)
   candy tuft

sempervirens (sem-per-vy'renz)
   evergreen

EVERGREEN CANDYTUFT

Family Cruciferae

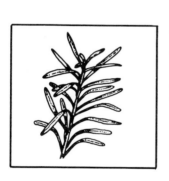

Zones	6, 7, 8.
Size	Height 6-10 inches; spread 1-2 feet.
Form	Rounded mounds. Foliage – alternate, 1 inch long, narrow. Flower – late March to early May; small umbels, 1 inch in diameter.
Texture	Fine.
Color	Foliage – dark green. Flower – white.
Culture	Sun. Soil – medium drainage; medium fertility. Moisture – medium. Pruning – shear after flowering. Pest Problems – none. Growth Rate – moderate.
Landscape Notes	Excellent ground cover for edging. Effective in rockeries. Named varieties often more compact.
Varieties	'Christmas Snow' – blooms again in fall. 'Purity' – very low spreading mound; neat in appearance. 'Snowflake' – stems and leaves larger and thicker than species.

Juniperus (jew-nip'er-us)
    juniperlike

chinensis (chi-nen'sis)
    from China

sargentii (sar-jent'ee-eye)
    named for C.S. Sargent,
    first director of Arnold Arboretum

SARGENT JUNIPER

Family Cupressaceae

Zones	6, 7, 8.
Size	Height 1 foot; spread 6-8 feet.
Form	Low spreading, forming broad mat with procumbent stems. Foliage – needlelike, opposite on many conspicuous twigs. Fruit – fall; ¼ -⅓ inch across, 2-5 seeded.
Texture	Fine.
Color	Foliage – steel blue. Fruit – brownish-violet.
Culture	Sun. Soil – good drainage; low fertility. Moisture – low. Pruning – none. Pest Problems – mites, bagworms, and scale. Growth Rate – moderate.
Landscape Notes	Best variety for adverse conditions. Withstands heat and salt spray. Effective in raised planters.

Juniperus (jew-nip'er-us)
   juniperlike

conferta (kon-fer'ta)
   crowded, pressed
   together

SHORE JUNIPER

Family Cupressaceae

Zones	6, 7, 8.
Size	Height 12-18 inches; spread 3-5 feet.
Form	Spreading with medium density. More open in growth than Andorra or Sargent Juniper and more vigorous. Foliage – needles to ½ inch long, usually in 3's. Fruit – fall; berrylike, ½ inch diameter.
Texture	Fine.
Color	Foliage – gray-green with white line on top. Fruit – black.
Culture	Sun but will tolerate part shade. Soil – good drainage; low fertility; prefers sandy loam. Moisture – low. Pruning – none. Pest Problems – red spiders. Growth Rate – rapid.
Landscape Notes	Drapes well on banks or in planters. Will grow on beach dunes or in clay. Spreads rapidly by underground stems. Effective in masses. Useful as foreground for taller plantings. Withstands severe exposure.
Variety	'Blue Pacific' – more compact; withstands heat well.

Juniperus (jew-nip'er-us)
    juniperlike

horizontalis (hor-ri-zon-tay'lis)
    horizontal

CREEPING JUNIPER

Family Cupressaceae

Zones	6, 7, 8.
Size	Height 12-18 inches; spread 3-5 feet.
Form	Low and open. Foliage – needlelike. Fruit – fall; berries ⅜ inch diameter, 1-4 seeds.
Texture	Fine.
Color	Foliage – bluish-green; winter, rust-green. Fruit – blue.
Culture	Sun. Soil – good drainage; low fertility; prefers slightly alkaline conditions. Moisture – low. Pruning – none. Pest Problems – bagworms and mites. Growth Rate – moderate to rapid.
Landscape Notes	Serviceable for difficult locations. Named varieties more colorful and interesting in habit of growth than species. Withstands city conditions.
Varieties	'Bar Harbor' – dwarf form; slow growing and very hardy. Blue-green foliage. 'Douglasii' – trailing form with blue-gray foliage turning pale purple in fall; rapid growth. Waukegan Juniper.

Liriope (li-ri'o-pe)
  lily-turf

muscarii (mus-cay'ree)
  grape hyacinth; from Latin
  for musky, in allusion to
  musky scent

LILY-TURF
Family Liliaceae

Zones	6, 7, 8.
Size	Height 6-12 inches; spread 12-18 inches.
Form	Grasslike with leaves recurving toward ground. Forms clumps. Foliage – 1-2 feet long and ⅓-1 inch wide. Flower – July to August; small clusters on center spike above leaves. Fruit – fall; berrylike in clusters.
Texture	Medium.
Color	Foliage – dark green. Flower – lavender-pink. Fruit – shiny black.
Culture	Shade but tolerates full sun. Soil – tolerant. Moisture – medium. Pruning – each March cut tops to within 3 inches of ground with lawn mower or by hand shearing. Pest Problems – scale. Growth Rate – moderate to rapid.
Landscape Notes	Thrives in practically any situation and is often used to border walks and drives. Frequently used in beds around trunks of trees. Effective in mass. Requires little care. Withstands salt spray.
Varieties	'Monroe White' – white flowers; shade only. *variegata* – leaves yellow-striped.

Liriope (li-ri'o-pe)
 lily-turf

spicata (spy-ka'ta)
 spiked; or having
 flowers in spike

CREEPING LILYTURF

Family Liliaceae

Zones	6, 7, 8.
Size	Height 6-10 inches; spread indeterminate.
Form	Grasslike with leaves recurving toward ground. Foliage – 13-15 inches long and ¼ inch wide. Flower – July to August; small clusters on center spike above leaves. Fruit – fall; berrylike.
Texture	Fine.
Color	Foliage – dark green. Flower – pale lilac or nearly white. Fruit – black.
Culture	Shade but tolerates sun. Soil – tolerant. Moisture – medium. Pruning – none. Pest Problems – scale. Growth Rate – rapid.
Landscape Notes	Excellent for preventing soil erosion. Withstands neglect when established; maintains neat appearance all seasons. Better cover than L. muscarii because of small size and faster suckering habit.

Ophiopogon (o-fi-o-po'gon)
Greek snake's beard

jaburan (jab'ur-ran)
oriental vernacular name

vittata (vit-tay'ta)
striped

SNAKEBEARD

Family Liliaceae

Zones	6, 7, 8.
Size	Height 8-12 inches; spread indeterminate.
Form	Grasslike with leaves recurving toward ground. Foliage – ¼ - ½ inch wide, 12-18 inches long, oblong lanceolate. Flower – small clusters on center spike usually hidden by foliage. Fruit – berrylike.
Texture	Medium.
Color	Foliage – green with white stripes. Flower – white to lilac. Fruit – dark blue.
Culture	Shade or sun. Soil – tolerant; good drainage; medium fertility. Moisture – medium; withstands drought well. Pruning – cut leaves to 1 inch in March with shears or mower. Pest Problems – none. Growth Rate – rapid.
Landscape Notes	Most attractive planted in small masses. Often used as border for flower beds and walks or thick plantings on gently sloping banks. Attractive in containers. Not as hardy as Liriope. Withstands salt spray. Little care required.
Varieties	*aureus* – yellow-striped leaves. 'Sunproof' – tolerates full sun.

Ophiopogon (o-fi-o-po'gon)
  Greek snake's beard

japonicus (ja-pon'i-kus)
  from Japan

MONDO GRASS

Family Liliaceae

Zones	6, 7, 8.
Size	Height 6-10 inches; spread indeterminate.
Form	Stemless clumps spreading to form grasslike cover. Foliage – grassy, 9-12 inches long and ⅛ inch wide, curving toward ground. Flower – July; tiny spikes usually hidden by foliage. Fruit – berrylike.
Texture	Fine.
Color	Foliage – dark green. Flower – pale lilac to white. Fruit – blue.
Culture	Sun or shade. Soil – good drainage; medium fertility with humus added. Moisture – medium. Pruning – none. Pest Problems – none. Growth Rate – rapid.
Landscape Notes	Resistant to drought and cold. Excellent cover for large or small areas; especially useful under trees. Set plants 4-6 inches apart or 3 inches in heavy shade. Excellent control of erosion when well established.

Pachysandra (pack-i-san'dra)
  evergreen

terminalis (ter-mi-nall'is)
  at end

JAPANESE SPURGE

Family Buxaceae

Zones	6, 7.
Size	Height 5-12 inches; spread indeterminate.
Form	Low and stoloniferous with matted, creeping rootstalks. Fleshy, erect stems with leaves tufted at top, forming loose carpets. Foliage – alternate, wedge-shaped to 2 inches long in clusters. Flower – midspring; inconspicuous terminal spikes. Fruit – summer; 3-horned drupe, ⅓ inch diameter.
Texture	Medium.
Color	Foliage – olive green. Flower – white. Fruit – white.
Culture	Shade. Soil – tolerant. Moisture – medium. Pruning – pinching tops in spring makes plants thicker. Pest Problems – scale and stem rot. Growth Rate – slow to moderate.
Landscape Notes	Excellent ground cover for shade. Of uniform height. Most effective planted thickly. Good texture accent on level ground under trees where grass will not grow. Blends well with plants of yellow or yellow-green coloration. Spreads by underground stolons. Does not grow well in warm areas.
Variety	*variegata* – leaves marked with white.

Phlox (flocks)
   showy garden plant

subulata (sub-you-lay′ta)
   awl-shaped

THRIFT

Family Polemoniaceae

Zones	6,7,8.
Size	Height 2-4 inches; spread indeterminate.
Form	Dense and creeping, forming mounds of foliage merging into solid carpet. Foliage – opposite, ½ inch long, awl-shaped, crowded. Flower – March to May; covering foliage, ¾ inch diameter.
Texture	Fine.
Color	Foliage – yellow green. Flower – white, pink, blue, or purple.
Culture	Sun. Soil – good drainage; medium to low fertility. Moisture – low. Pruning – none. Pest Problems – fairly clean. Growth Rate – moderate.
Landscape Notes	Good for use in rock gardens, borders, and on small banks. Valued for ability to survive under adverse conditions. May be used as soil stabilizer. Useful in mass for ground cover. Best in small areas. Colors other than rose-crimson blend better with surroundings. Little care required after establishment except division every 3 or 4 years.
Varieties	*alba* – white flowers. 'Alexander's Pink' – pink flowers. 'Emerald Cushion' – pink flowers, habit dwarf and compact.

Rosa (ro'za)
old Latin name
for rose

wichuraiana (wy-shur-a‧an'a)
in honor of Wichuray,
Russian botanist

MEMORIAL ROSE

Family Rosaceae

Zones	6, 7, 8.
Size	Height 1-2 feet; spread 20 feet or more.
Form	Dense, creeping, and prostrate sending out long trailing shoots. Foliage – alternate, 7-9 oval leaflets 2-3 inches long. Flower – May; single or semidouble in fragrant corymbs about 2 inches across. Fruit – late summer; ovoid hips.
Texture	Medium.
Color	Foliage – dark green. Flower – white. Fruit – red.
Culture	Sun or part shade. Soil – fairly tolerant. Moisture – medium. Pruning – cut out dead or weak wood; fasten stolons for cover. Pest Problems – fire blight. Growth Rate – rapid.
Landscape Notes	Beautiful cover for banks in full sun and rockeries. Roots along procumbent stems and aids in erosion control. Good barrier planting; may be trained on fence for screen.
Varieties	'Evangeline' – large clusters of soft-pink fragrant flowers. 'Phyllis Bide' – small buff-yellow flowers.

Santolina (san-to-ly'na)
lavender cotton, aromatic
undershrubs

chamaecyparissus (kam-ee-sip-a-ris'sus)
Greek for dwarf cypress

LAVENDER-COTTON

Family Compositae

Zones	6, 7, 8.
Size	Height 1-2 feet; spread 3-4 feet.
Form	Very dense and compact low-spreading mounds. Foliage – alternate, ½ inch long, aromatic. Flower – June; buttonlike, ½ - ¾ inch diameter.
Texture	Fine.
Color	Foliage – silvery gray-green. Flower – yellow.
Culture	Sun. Soil – very good drainage; low fertility. Moisture – low. Pruning – remove top growth to crown every 2 to 3 years for renewal; remove flowers annually. Pest Problems – fungus during damp seasons. Growth Rate – moderate.
Landscape Notes	For foliage effect in rock gardens and foreground planting. Will not tolerate wet soil or high fertilization. Highly aromatic foliage. Useful on poor, sandy, or gravelly soils. Stems root where they touch ground. Somewhat salt tolerant.

Santolina (san-to-ly'na)
   lavender cotton, aromatic
   undershrubs

virens (vy'renz)
   green

GREEN SANTOLINA

Family Compositae

Zones	6, 7, 8.
Size	Height 12-18 inches; spread 2-3 feet.
Form	Very dense mounds. Foliage – alternate, pinnate, aromatic, 1-2 inches long and ¹⁄₁₆ inch wide. Flower – summer; buttonlike, ⅝ inch.
Texture	Fine.
Color	Foliage – emerald green. Flower – yellow.
Culture	Sun. Soil – very good drainage; low fertility. Moisture – low. Pruning – remove top growth to crown every 2 to 3 years for renewal; remove flowers annually. Pest Problems – excess moisture may cause fungus. Growth Rate – moderate.
Landscape Notes	Excellent for mass or border plantings. For foliage effect in rock gardens. May be clipped to form dwarf hedge. Useful in poor, sandy or gravelly soils. Foliage aromatic.

Sarcococca (sar-ko-kok'a)
  Greek for flesh and berry

hookeriana (hook-er-i-a'na)
  named for J.D. Hooker

humilis (hu'mi-lis)
  dwarf or low-growing

SMALL HIMALAYAN
SARCOCOCCA

Family Buxaceae

Zones	6, 7, 8.
Size	Height 1-2 feet; spread 1½-2½ feet.
Form	Loose and informal. Foliage – alternate, entire, 1-2 inches. Flower – inconspicuous. Fruit – round, ⅓ inch diameter, inconspicuous.
Texture	Medium.
Color	Foliage – lustrous dark green. Flower – white. Fruit – blue-black. Stem – green.
Culture	Part shade. Soil – medium drainage; medium fertility with humus added. Moisture – medium to low. Pruning – remove dead wood. Pest Problems – none. Growth Rate – moderate.
Landscape Notes	Useful in groups as filler and background, as informal border, or as ground cover.

Teucrium (too'kri-um)
   named for King Teucer,
   first king of Troy

chamaedrys (kam-ee'dris)
   pre-Linnaean name for
   some germander

GERMANDER

Family Labiatae

Zones	6, 7, 8.
Size	Height 10-12 inches; spread 8-10 inches.
Form	Irregularly spreading mounds with moderate branching. Foliage opposite, small, dense, arranged in whorls. Flower – late summer; ¾ inch long on showy spikes.
Texture	Medium to fine.
Color	Foliage – very pubescent, giving grayish color to dark green leaves. Flower – rose-purple.
Culture	Sun. Soil – good drainage; medium fertility. Moisture – medium. Pruning – shear after flowering if dwarf hedge desired. Pest Problems – none. Growth Rate – moderate.
Landscape Notes	Fine border plant suitable for rock and herb gardens, formal and informal edgings. Useful for summer bloom in front of evergreens.
Variety	*prostratum* – to 8 inches. Flowers heavily.

Vinca (vin'ka)
   periwinkle, creeping myrtle

major (ma'jor)
   greater, larger

BIG PERIWINKLE

Family Apocynaceae

Zones	6, 7.
Size	Height 1 foot; spread indeterminate.
Form	Upright and more open and loose than *V. minor.* Foliage – opposite, 3 inches long. Flower – March and April; 1-2 inches wide.
Texture	Medium.
Color	Foliage – glossy light green. Flower – light blue.
Culture	Sun or shade; competition from weeds in sun. Soil – very tolerant. Moisture – low. Pruning – needs some clipping. Pest Problems – fungus in fertile soils. Growth Rate – rapid.
Landscape Notes	Excellent for naturalizing. Good ground cover for banks; can compete with worst root conditions under trees. Suitable for window boxes. Requires little maintenance.
Variety	*variegata* – cream-colored markings on leaves.

Vinca (vin'ka)
   periwinkle,
   creeping myrtle

minor (my'nor)
   smaller

PERIWINKLE

Family Apocynaceae

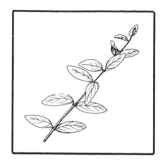

Zones	6, 7.
Size	Height 5-8 inches; spread 3-4 feet.
Form	Wide-spreading with stems rooting along ground, non-climbing, medium density. Foliage – opposite, 1-2 inches long. Flower – March and April; single, ¾ inch diameter.
Texture	Medium.
Color	Foliage – lustrous dark green. Flower – blue.
Culture	Part shade or shade; competition from grass in sun. Soil – medium drainage; low fertility. Moisture – low to medium. Pruning – crowded, neglected plantings improved by severe thinning to increase vigor. Pest Problems – stem canker, fungus in fertile soils. Growth Rate – rapid.
Landscape Notes	Excellent ground cover under trees and for covering shady banks. Usually more desirable ground cover than *V. major*. Roots along stems to make new plants.
Varieties	'Alba' – white flowers. 'Alpinia' – large blue flowers. 'Bowles Variety' – flowers light blue, vigorous growth.

GROUND COVERS — DECIDUOUS

Hemerocallis (hem-er-o-kal'is)
   from Greek meaning
   beautiful for one day

hybrida (hy'brid-a)
   hybrid

DAYLILY HYBRIDS

Family Liliaceae

Zones	6, 7, 8.
Size	Height – foliage 18 inches, scape to 5 feet; spread 3-4 feet.
Form	Herbaceous perennial spreading from crown by fleshy rhizomes. Foliage – 2 feet long, 1 ⅓ inches wide. Flower – summer; 5 inches long and 3½ inches wide, 6-12 on tall scapes, not fragrant.
Texture	Medium to coarse.
Color	Foliage – light green. Flower – yellow, orange, dark red, pink, and combinations.
Culture	Sun or shade. Soil – tolerant; prefers loam. Moisture – very tolerant. Pruning – remove scapes after flowering. Pest Problems – none. Growth Rate – rapid.
Landscape Notes	Select evergreen varieties whenever possible; mulch until established. Inexpensive species useful in masses for large scale or roadside plantings and to control erosion on banks and near water. Will grow in difficult areas with minimum care. Space 1½-3 feet apart. More than 12,000 varieties now grown.

Hosta (hos'ta)
    plantain lily

lancifolia (lan-si-fo'li-a)
    lance-shaped leaves

NARROW-LEAVED
PLANTAIN LILY

Family Liliaceae

Zones	6, 7, 8.
Size	Height 1½-2 feet; spread 4 feet.
Form	Perennial herb forming clumps. Foliage – slender, lanceolate, 6 inches long, 1½-2 inches wide, tapering at both ends. Flower – August; 2 inches long, bell-shaped on scapes.
Texture	Coarse.
Color	Foliage – dark green. Flower – lilac or pale lavender.
Culture	Shade or part shade. Soil – tolerant if fertile. Moisture – high. Pruning – remove dead foliage in winter. Pest Problems – slugs. Growth Rate – rapid.
Landscape Notes	Low maintenance perennial beautiful in foliage and flower as specimen or border plant. Plant close together for immediate covering under trees. Most useful massed or in planter boxes. Many other species equally attractive.
Varieties	'Albo-marginata' – margins of leaves white. *tardiflora* – autumn flowering.

Hosta (hos'ta)
　　plantain lily

plantaginea (plan-ta-ji-nee'uh)
　　unexplained

FRAGRANT PLANTAIN

Family Liliaceae

Zones	6, 7, 8.
Size	Height 1½-2½ feet; spread 4 feet.
Form	Perennial herb forming clumps. Foliage – 4-5 inches wide, 6 inches long on stem to 2 feet long. Flower – late summer; 4 inches long, fragrant, on scapes 1½-2½ feet above foliage.
Texture	Coarse.
Color	Foliage – green. Flower – white.
Culture	Part shade. Soil – medium drainage; high to medium fertility. Moisture – high. Pruning – remove dead foliage. Pest Problems – none. Growth Rate – rapid.
Landscape Notes	Excellent for bordering walks and drives in shaded areas or as specimen. Only *Hosta* with scented flowers.

VINES — EVERGREEN

Akebia (a-kee'bi-a)
   Asian woody vines

quinata (kwi-na'ta)
   in fives

FIVELEAF AKEBIA

Family Lardizabalaceae

Zones	6, 7, 8.
Size	Height 30-40 feet; spread indeterminate.
Form	Climbs by twining. Foliage – alternate, 5 leaflets palmately compound, each 2 inches long. Flower – April to May; ½-1 inch diameter in clusters, fragrant. Fruit – 2-3 inch pods.
Texture	Medium to fine.
Color	Foliage – pale to medium green; winter, purplish. Flower – purple. Fruit – purple.
Culture	Sun or light shade. Soil – good drainage; medium to low fertility. Moisture – low. Pruning – control growth to desired height. Pest Problems – none. Growth Rate – rapid.
Landscape Notes	Excellent foliage for fences or trellis if carefully controlled. Spreads by long underground runners. May lose some leaves in severe winters.

Anisostichus (an-i-sos-tic'us)
   unexplained

capreolatus (kap-re-a-lay'tus)
   winding, turning

CROSSVINE

Family Bignoniaceae

Zones	6, 7, 8.
Size	Height 50-60 feet; spread indeterminate.
Form	Climbs by tendrils. Foliage – opposite and compound, 2 leaflets to 6 inches long, terminal tendrils, entire, stiff. Flower – mid-April; trumpet-shaped, 2 inches wide. Fruit – July; pods 1 foot long.
Texture	Coarse.
Color	Foliage – dark green, glabrous; winter, purplish. Flower – orange-red. Fruit – green turning brown.
Culture	Sun for best flowering. Soil – tolerant; prefers loam. Moisture – medium. Pruning – train. Pest Problems – none. Growth Rate – rapid.
Landscape Notes	Excellent fast-growing screen for wire fences and can be trained on masonry walls. Grown for handsome foliage and flower production. Formerly named *Bignonia capreolata*.
Variety	*atro-sanguinea* – flowers dark purple. Leaves longer and narrower than species.

Clematis (klem'a-tis)
 woody flowering vines

armandii (ar-man'dye)
 unexplained

ARMAND CLEMATIS

Family Ranunculaceae

Zone	7.
Size	Height 15-20 feet; spread indeterminate.
Form	Climbs by twisting petioles. Foliage – 5 inches wide with 3 leaflets, linear and entire. Flower – spring; 1-2½ inches in showy panicles, fragrant, blooms on growth of previous year.
Texture	Coarse.
Color	Foliage – medium to glossy green. Flower – white.
Culture	Sun for top growth, cool shade over roots. Soil – fertile; neutral to alkaline. Moisture – medium to low. Pruning – mid-summer after bloom if necessary. Pest Problems – clematis borer, leaf spot, and root rot. Growth Rate – rapid.
Landscape Notes	Prefers cool areas. Fast-growing with beautiful flowers; use as accent to cover pergolas and trellises. Does not tolerate cultivation.
Variety	'Farquhariana' – light pink flowers.

Euonymus (you-on'i-mus)
   hardy shrubs and vines

fortunei (for-too'nee-i)
   named for Robert Fortune

WINTERCREEPER

Family Celastraceae

Zones	6. 7, 8.
Size	Height 3-6 feet when clinging to wall; spread 2-4 feet.
Form	Vinelike, climbing by aerial roots on solid surfaces. Foliage – opposite, ¼-2 inches long.
Texture	Medium.
Color	Foliage – dark green with whitish veins; fall, reddish. Stem – green.
Culture	Sun or shade. Soil – medium drainage; medium fertility with high organic content. Moisture – medium to high. Pruning – thin. Pest Problems – scale and aphids on new growth. Growth Rate – moderate.
Landscape Notes	Desirable as low screen against masonry or tree trunks, and may be used as low ground cover for difficult situations in shade or with poor drainage. Tolerates salt spray. Excellent as bank cover. Allows little weed competition.
Varieties	'Coloratus' – 1 inch leaves which turn reddish-purple in winter. 'Kewensis' – ¼ inch leaves; slow growing, use in small areas. 'Minimus' – 1½ inch leaves. *radicans* – 1 inch leaves.

Fatshedera (fats-hed'e-ra)
    bigeneric hybrid; English
    ivy and Fatsia japonica

lizei (li-ze'i)
    unexplained

BUSHIVY

Family Araliaceae

Zones	7, 8.
Size	Height 8-9 feet; spread indeterminate.
Form	Vinelike, requires support. Foliage – alternate, starfish in shape reaching 10 inches in width on established plants. Palmately 5-lobed. Flower – fall, 1 inch spherical heads. Fruit – berry on old wood.
Texture	Coarse.
Color	Foliage – dark lustrous green. Flower – pale green. Fruit – blue. Stem – green.
Culture	Shade or part shade with protection in Piedmont and mountains. Soil – tolerant; good drainage; medium fertility. Moisture – medium to low. Pruning – train or confine. Pest Problems – aphids. Growth Rate – rapid.
Landscape Notes	Excellent espalier plant. Outstanding for use in exterior and interior planter boxes. Good filler in narrow strips between walk and wall. Tolerates beach conditions if protected from strong winds. Plant in protected areas west of coastal regions.

Ficus (fy'kus)
    classical Latin
    for fig

pumila (pew'mi-la)
    dwarf, small

CLIMBING FIG

Family Moraceae

Zone	8.
Size	Height to 30 feet; spread indeterminate.
Form	Climbs by aerial rootlets with leaves held flat against wall. Foliage – alternate, simple, entire; juvenile leaves about 1 inch long, mature leaves 2-4 inches long. Fruit – 2 inch figs on older plants; inedible.
Texture	Fine to medium.
Color	Foliage – light green. Fruit – yellowish-green.
Culture	Part shade or shade. Soil – tolerant. Moisture – medium. Pruning – remove young, erect growth and cut back old main stems to forestall maturity. Pest Problems – harbors insects in dense mat if not thinned. Growth Rate – rapid.
Landscape Notes	Very good for covering masonry walls. Avoid planting near wood construction. Forms lacy pattern of stems and foliage over support until completely covered. Not hardy in Piedmont or mountains.
Varieties	'Minima' – dwarf climbing fig. 'Variegata' – small green and white leaves; pointed.

Gelsemium (gel-see'mi-um)
Latin version of jessamine

sempervirens (sem-per-vy'renz)
evergreen

CAROLINA JESSAMINE

Family Loganiaceae

Zones	6, 7, 8.
Size	Height to 20 feet; spread indeterminate.
Form	Twining vine with wiry thin stems; growth becoming stockier with generous exposure to sun. Delicate growth character. Foliage – opposite, narrow and pointed, small and waxy. Flower – late February to early April; fragrant, single or in small cymes. Fruit – flattened winged capsule.
Texture	Fine.
Color	Foliage – shiny dark green; winter, wine-red. Flower – yellow. Fruit – brown.
Culture	Sun or shade. Soil – tolerant. Moisture – medium. Pruning – shear after flowering. Pest Problems – none. Growth Rate – moderate; rapid when established.
Landscape Notes	Good screening material. Flower production best in sun. Grows well on fences and trellises; train first growth horizontally to cover wire. Will climb on small trees and down spouts. Native to Southeast.
Variety	'Plena' – double flowered.

Hedera (hed'er-a)
  classical name of ivy

canariensis (ka-nay-ri-en'sis)
  from Canary Islands

ALGERIAN IVY

Family Araliaceae

Zones	7,8.
Size	Height to 30 feet; spread indeterminate.
Form	Mass of trailing vines climbing by aerial roots. Foliage – alternate, thick and leathery, 5-7 lobed, 2-6 inches long, 3-5 inches wide. Fruit – berry.
Texture	Coarse.
Color	Foliage – glossy dark green. Fruit – blue-black. Twigs – green when young, red when older.
Culture	Shade. Soil – tolerant; good drainage; medium fertility. Moisture – medium to high. Pruning – none. Pest Problems – snails and scale insects. Growth Rate – moderate to rapid.
Landscape Notes	Must be confined if used in small garden. Easy and inexpensive to establish. May be used as ground cover. Not cold hardy in mountain areas.
Varieties	'Canary Cream' – green leaves with cream-colored margins. 'Shamrock' – for small, refined areas.

Hedera (hed'er-a)
classical name of ivy

colchica (kol'chi-ka)
from Colchis, ancient
name of region of N. E.
shore of Black Sea

COLCHIS IVY

Family Araliaceae

Zones	6, 7.
Size	Height of 30 feet; spread indeterminate.
Form	Mass of vines clinging by aerial roots. Foliage – alternate, heart-shaped and thick, very slightly 3-lobed, 2-6 inches long, fragrant when crushed. Fruit – berrylike.
Texture	Coarse.
Color	Foliage – dark green. Fruit – black.
Culture	Shade. Soil – very tolerant. Moisture – **medium**. Pruning – thin. Pest Problems – aphids. Growth Rate – moderate.
Landscape Notes	Useful on fences or as accent. May be sheared to form topiary object. Can be used as ground cover. Must be confined if used in small garden.

Hedera (hed'er-a)
    classical name of ivy

helix (he'licks)
    Latin for ivy

ENGLISH IVY

Family Araliaceae

Zones	6, 7, 8.
Size	Height to 50 feet; spread indeterminate.
Form	Climbs on solid surfaces by aerial roots; dense. Foliage – alternate, to 4 inches long with 3-5 lobes, margins entire. Flower – inconspicuous. Fruit – berry.
Texture	Medium to coarse.
Color	Foliage – dark green with gray veins. Fruit – bluish-black.
Culture	Part shade to shade. Soil – medium drainage; medium fertility with high organic content. Moisture – medium to high. Pruning – needs control to prevent damage to wood trim or siding. Pest Problems – scale, aphids, mealybug, fungus leaf spot, and bacterial leaf spot under moist conditions. Growth Rate – rapid once established.
Landscape Notes	May be used as ground cover; should not be permitted to grow in valuable trees. Aggressive in adapted conditions. Numerous small-leaved forms available for limited ground areas. Variegated foliage types also in nursery trade. Easy and inexpensive to establish. Some low temperature injury in mountains.
Varieties	'Aureo-variegata' – leaves variegated yellow. *baltica* – small-leaved form, very hardy. 'Gracilis' – small leaves turning bronze in winter.

Jasminum (jas'min-um)
Arabic name for jasmine

officinale (of-fish-i-na'lee)
medicinal

COMMON JASMINE

Family Oleaceae

Zones	7, 8.
Size	Height to 15 feet; spread indeterminate.
Form	Semi-climbing and shrublike requiring support. Foliage – opposite, pinnate, 5-7 pairs of leaflets each ½ to 2 inches long. Flower – late spring and summer; ¾-1 inch wide in clusters, fragrant. Fruit – 2-lobed berry.
Texture	Medium.
Color	Foliage – green. Flower – white. Fruit – black.
Culture	Sun or part shade. Soil – tolerant. Moisture – tolerant. Pruning – none. Pest Problems – none. Growth Rate – moderate.
Landscape Notes	Popular for summer flowers and fragrance. Useful on arbors or trellises, having graceful, airy effect.
Varieties	*aureo-variegatum* – variegated leaves. *grandiflorum* – flowers larger and more showy, to 1½ inches wide.

Lonicera (lon-iss'er-a)
   honeysuckles

sempervirens (sem-per-vi'renz)
   evergreen

TRUMPET HONEYSUCKLE

Family Caprifoliaceae

Zones	6, 7, 8.
Size	Height 50 feet; spread indeterminate.
Form	Twining vine. Foliage – opposite, thin, 1½-3 inches long, perfoliate. Flower – mid-April through summer; trumpet-shaped, 2 inches long. Fruit – fall; berries ⅛-¼ inch diameter.
Texture	Medium.
Color	Foliage – gray-green. Flower – gold to scarlet red. Fruit – translucent red.
Culture	Sun to part shade. Soil – tolerant. Moisture – tolerant. Pruning – maintain desired size. Pest Problems – aphids. Growth Rate – rapid.
Landscape Notes	Excellent for naturalizing. Begins bloom with dogwood and continues throughout summer if grown in sun. Flowers and foliage interesting at close range on trellis or fence.
Varieties	'Magnifica' – bright scarlet flowers; late flowering. 'Sulphurea' – yellow flowers. 'Superba' – bright scarlet flowers.

Rosa (ro'za)
old Latin name
for rose

banksiae (banks-i'a)
named for
Lady Banks

BANKS ROSE

Family Rosaceae

Zones	7, 8.
Size	Height 10-20 feet; spread indeterminate.
Form	Requires support for climbing. Foliage – alternate, 3 to 5 leaflets, 1½-2½ inches long. shining, glabrous. Flower – April to May; single or double on slender smooth pedicels in many flowered umbels, about 1 inch diameter, slightly fragrant. Stem – nearly thornless.
Texture	Fine.
Color	Foliage – deep green. Flower – white or creamy yellow. Stems – new growth green.
Culture	Sun or part shade. Soil – tolerant. Moisture – medium. Pruning – train. Pest Problems – none. Growth Rate – rapid.
Landscape Notes	Forms good screen; has numerous flowers. Needs space for massive growth and must be trained to support. Requires little maintenance. Tolerates salt spray. Not reliably hardy in mountains.
Varieties	'Alba-plena' – very fragrant white double flowers.
	'Lutea' – double yellow flowers.
	'Lutescens' – single yellow flowers.
	'Normalis' – single white flowers.

Smilax (smi'laks)
ancient Greek
name of obscure
meaning

lanceolata (lan-see-o-lay'ta)
shaped like lance head

SMILAX

Family Liliaceae

Zones	6, 7, 8.
Size	Height 20-30 feet; spread indeterminate.
Form	Climbing by extending tendrils. Foliage – alternate, simple, 2-6 inches long, ovate or rounded with broadly heart-shaped base. Fruit – berry.
Texture	Medium.
Color	Foliage – shining bright green. Fruit –·dark red.
Culture	Sun or shade. Soil – tolerant. Moisture – medium. Pruning – should be heavily pruned annually in December. Pest Problems – none. Growth Rate – rapid.
Landscape Notes	Handsome foliage frequently used in bouquets and Christmas decorations. Forms dense screen on trellises and fences. Excellent vine that should be more widely used. Spreads by underground shoots.

Trachelospermum (trak-ee-lo-sperm'um)
  star jasmine

asiaticum (a-shi-at'i-kum)
  of Asia

YELLOW STAR-JASMINE

Family Apocynaceae

Zones	7,8.
Size	Height to 12 feet; spread to 15 feet.
Form	Climbs by twining. Foliage – opposite, 3 inches. Flower – May and June; ¾ inch wide, star-shaped, very fragrant.
Texture	Medium.
Color	Foliage – dark glossy green; new growth reddish-brown. Flower – pale yellow.
Culture	Part shade. Soil – medium drainage; high fertility. Moisture – high to medium. Pruning – shape. Pest Problems – scale and white fly. Growth Rate – slow to moderate.
Landscape Notes	Somewhat more cold hardy than *T. jasminoides*. For spot interest on fences and walls where fragrance may be appreciated. Elegant and interesting foliage.
Variety	*oblanceolatum* – smaller leaves and more cold hardy.

VINES — DECIDUOUS

Actinidia (ak-tin-id'ia)
from Greek for ray,
referring to radiate styles

chinensis (chi-nen'sis)
from China

KIWI VINE

Family Dilleniaceae

Zones	7, 8.
Size	Height 25 feet; spread 30 feet.
Form	Climbs by twining. Foliage – alternate, 5-8 inches long and 4-7 inches wide. Flower – May; inconspicuous, sexes separate. Fruit – summer; globular berry 1½ inch diameter, edible.
Texture	Coarse.
Color	Foliage – medium to yellow-green with prominent red hairs on new shoots. Flower – white. Fruit – brownish green, hairy.
Culture	Sun or part shade. Soil – medium drainage; medium to high fertility. Moisture – medium. Pruning – none or as needed to maintain size. Pest Problems – none. Growth Rate – rapid.
Landscape Notes	Grown mainly for luxuriant effect of foliage but also bears delicious fruit. Use as texture contrast in large scale areas or as accent plant for pergolas and trellises. Plant staminate and pistillate plants if fruits desired.

Clematis (klem'a-tis)
   woody flowering vines

hybrida (hy'brid-a)
   hybrid

LARGE-FLOWERED CLEMATIS

Family Ranunculaceae

Zones	6,7,8.
Size	Height 5-30 feet; spread indeterminate.
Form	Climbs by twining; woody, fragile stems. Foliage – opposite, compound, 3-8 leaflets. Flower – late spring through early summer; large and solitary, or few flowers in clusters or small flowers in profuse clusters, 2 to 10 inches in diameter; single or double.
Texture	Medium to fine.
Color	Foliage – bright green. Flower – white, red, purple, blue, or lavender.
Culture	Sun for top growth, cool shade over roots. Soil – good drainage; medium high fertility; prefers rich loam. Moisture – high. Pruning – sometimes required to train and to increase flower production. Pest Problems – stem rot. Growth Rate – moderate.
Landscape Notes	Easily trained to wall or form. Requires care throughout year. Restrained and delicate growth habit. Weak climber. Best in Piedmont or mountain regions.
Varieties	'Belle of Woking' – double silvery gray flowers; prune after flowering. 'Comptesse de Bouchard' – satiny rose flowers, 5-6 inch diameter; prune in early spring.

Clematis (klem'a-tis)
   woody flowering vines

paniculata (pan-ick-kew-lay'ta)
   compound raceme

JAPANESE CLEMATIS

Family Ranunculaceae

Zones	6, 7, 8.
Size	Height to 30 feet; spread indeterminate.
Form	Dense and heavy; climbing by twining stems and petioles, forming thick tangle heaviest at top. Foliage – midspring to late fall; opposite, 3-5 entire or lobed leaflets, glabrous. Flower – late August; panicles of 1 inch flowers, light, lacy, with bitter-sweet odor. Fruit – fall, persisting; 1-seeded achenes, interesting fluffy seed head. Stem – slender, slightly downy.
Texture	Medium in foliage, but very fine with flowers and fruits.
Color	Foliage – bright green. Flower – white. Fruit – gray. Stem – gray.
Culture	Sun. Soil – good drainage; medium fertility. Moisture – high. Pruning – trim older stems to ground to promote foliage production. Annual pruning to thin out old wood. Pest Problems – spider mites and blister beetles. Growth Rate – rapid.
Landscape Notes	Valued for effect of flowers and fruits. Vigorous and easy to grow. Valuable as late blooming clematis for decorative screen. Will retain some leaves in winter. Blooms on current season's growth. Moderately resistant to salt spray. Grows well in cooler sections of Coastal Plains.

Clematis (klem'a-tis)
woody flowering vines

virginiana (vir-gin-i-a'na)
from Virginia

VIRGIN'S BOWER

Family Ranunculaceae

Zones	6, 7, 8.
Size	Height 12-15 feet; spread indeterminate.
Form	Climbs by twining stems and twining petioles; heavy at top with thin base. Foliage – very late spring to late fall; opposite, ovate leaflets 3-parted, some coarsely and unequally toothed. Flower – all summer; dioecious; small, profusely produced. Fruit – fall, persisting; achenes. Stem – younger growth ribbed, glabrous.
Texture	Medium in foliage, but very fine in bloom.
Color	Foliage – bright green; fall, purple. Flower – white. Fruit – gray. Stem – yellow-gray; young growth green.
Culture	Sun but will tolerate some shade. Soil – good drainage; medium fertility. Moisture – high. Pruning – train. Pest Problems – none. Growth Rate – moderate.
Landscape Notes	Commonly seen along creek banks and streams. Good for naturalized plantings. Valued for effect of fruit and flowers; also good foliage effect. Inferior to *C. paniculata*.

Hydrangea (hy-dran'jee-a)
   hardy shrubs, vines

anomala (a-nom'a-la)
   unusual or out of ordinary

petiolaris (pet-i-o-la'ris)
   with leaf stalk

CLIMBING HYDRANGEA

Family Saxifragaceae

Zones	6, 7, 8.
Size	Height to 50 feet; spread indeterminate.
Form	High climbing and producing heavy laterals from supporting surface. Climbs by aerial roots. Foliage – opposite, 2-4 inches with long, slender petioles. Flower – May; flat-topped clusters 6-10 inches wide, outer flowers of cluster sterile.
Texture	Coarse.
Color	Foliage – dark green, glabrous; fall, yellow. Flower – pure white. Bark – reddish, shredding.
Culture	Part shade. Soil – medium drainage; medium to high fertility with humus added. Moisture – high. Pruning – none unless restriction is desired. Pest Problems – none. Growth Rate – slow.
Landscape Notes	Clings to masonry and trees without support. Most suitable in rustic environments. Stems attractive in winter. Interesting effect on stone. Flowers only after mature. Does not bloom well in dense shade. Formerly named *H. petiolaris*.

Parthenocissus (par-thenn-o-sis'sus)
  Greek meaning virgin ivy

quinquefolia (kwin-kuh-fo'li-a)
  with 5 leaves or 5 leaflets

VIRGINIA CREEPER

Family Vitaceae

Zones	6, 7, 8.
Size	Height 10-20 feet; spread indeterminate.
Form	Climbs by tendrils with adhesive discs. Foliage – alternate, palmately divided into 5 leaflets to 6 inches long. Flower – inconspicuous. Fruit – fall; small berries.
Texture	Coarse.
Color	Foliage – glossy green; fall, brilliant red. Flower – white. Fruit – bluish-black.
Culture	Sun to part shade. Soil – very tolerant; medium drainage; medium fertility. Moisture – medium. Pruning – none. Pest Problems – Japanese beetles. Growth Rate – rapid.
Landscape Notes	Native to woods in Southeast. Most useful for large-scale work. Small-leaved varieties more refined in appearance than species. Widely adapted. Produces quick screen. Grown for rich foliage effect in summer and outstanding fall color. Resistant to salt spray. Where no support is available, makes dense ground cover. Birds attracted to fruit.
Varieties	*engelmannii* – small leaflets; well-suited to city gardens. *saint-paulii* – small leaflets; clings well to stone walls.

Parthenocissus (par-thenn-o-sis'sus)
 Greek meaning virgin ivy

tricuspidata (try-kus-pi-day'ta)
 having 3 points

BOSTON IVY

Family Vitaceae

Zones	6, 7, 8.
Size	Height up to 30 feet; spread indeterminate.
Form	Climbs by tendrils with adhesive discs. Foliage – alternate, 3-lobed to 8 inches wide. Flower – inconspicuous. Fruit – fall; small berries, inconspicuous.
Texture	Coarse.
Color	Foliage – glossy green; fall, red. Fruit – bluish-black.
Culture	Sun to part shade. Soil – tolerant; medium drainage; medium fertility. Moisture – medium. Pruning – needs periodic thinning. Pest Problems – scale, aphids on new shoots. Growth Rate – rapid.
Landscape Notes	Clings well on masonry work; small leaf varieties less vigorous. Withstands city conditions well. Cold hardy. Fall color not as outstanding as *P. quinquefolia*. Fruit attracts birds.
Varieties	'Lowii' – very small leaves; better suited to confined areas than species.
	'Veitchii' – very small leaves which are purple when young.

Rosa (ro'za)
    old Latin name
    for rose

hybrida (hy'brid-a)
    hybrid

CLIMBING ROSE

Family Rosaceae

Zones	6, 7, 8.
Size	Height 6-40 feet; spread indeterminate.
Form	Vigorous growing canes incapable of climbing unless trained on support. Foliage – alternate, usually 5 leaflets. Flower – May to August; 1-3 inch diameter.
Texture	Medium to fine.
Color	Foliage – deep glossy green. Flower – white, yellow, orange, pink, red, lavender, or bicolor.
Culture	Sun or part shade. Soil – good drainage; high fertility. Moisture – medium. Pruning – annually to train growth and to maintain vigor of plant. Pest Problems – less susceptible to disease and pests than bush roses; use all-purpose rose spray when necessary. Growth Rate – rapid.
Landscape Notes	Train to cover walls, fences, or trellises. Excellent as cover for chain-link fence. Will bloom better if trained in horizontal plane. Grown for flower effect.
Varieties	'Blaze' – scarlet-red flowers; vigorous, everblooming. 'Golden Showers' – yellow flowers; blooms almost continually.

Vitis (vy'tis)
   woody vines, grape

rotundifolia (ro-tun-di-fo'li-a)
   round-leaved

MUSCADINE GRAPE

Family Vitaceae

Zones	6, 7, 8.
Size	Height to 50 feet; spread indeterminate.
Form	Climbing by tendrils. Foliage – alternate, 3-6 inches wide, coarsely toothed. Flower – summer; inconspicuous. Fruit – early fall; small clusters, edible.
Texture	Coarse.
Color	Foliage – bright green; fall, green to lemon yellow depending on variety. Fruit – dull purple.
Culture	Sun. Soil – tolerant; good drainage; medium fertility. Moisture – medium. Pruning – annually. Pest Problems – spraying necessary for best fruit production. Growth Rate – rapid.
Landscape Notes	Plant perfect flowered varieties to insure pollination. Ideal summer screen. Fruit ripens in September and October. Grown for fruit, screening, and as ornament. Mildly tolerant to salt spray and sandy soil.
Varieties	'Albemarle' – black fruit; perfect flowered. 'Carlos' – bronze fruit; perfect flowered.

Wisteria (wis-ter'i-a)
    named for
    Casper Wistar

floribunda (flor-i-bun'da)
    blooming freely; floriferous

JAPANESE WISTERIA

Family Fabaceae

Zones	6, 7, 8.
Size	Height to 30 feet or more; spread indeterminate.
Form	Climbs by twining stems right to left, developing twisted woody trunk several inches in diameter. Foliage – early spring to fall; 13-19 pinnately compound leaflets. Flower – late spring; showy, pendent clusters 12-24 inches long, open from base to tip, fragrant. Fruit – fall; large velvety pods narrowed near base.
Texture	Medium.
Color	Foliage – bright green; fall, yellow. Flower – violet blue. Fruit – brown.
Culture	Sun. Soil – tolerant; medium drainage; medium fertility. Moisture – medium. Pruning – train. Pest Problems – aphids and scale. Growth Rate – moderate.
Landscape Notes	Large and very aggressive climber valued for flowers and foliage; useful on pergolas and trellises; may be trained as standard. Difficult to transplant. Rampant growth can girdle trees. Interesting trunk with age. Has longer blooming period than *W. sinensis.*
Varieties	*alba* – white flowers in dense clusters. 'Macrobotrys' – fragrant violet flowers in clusters 2-3 feet long. 'Rosea' – fragrant pink flowers.

Wisteria (wis-ter'i-a)
  named for Caspar Wistar

sinensis (sy-nen'sis)
  from China

CHINESE WISTERIA

Family Fabaceae

Zones	6, 7, 8.
Size	Height to 30 feet or more; spread indeterminate.
Form	Climbs by twining stems left to right; develops twisted woody trunk several inches in diameter. Foliage – early spring to midfall or late fall; 7-13 pinnately compound leaflets. Flower – early April before leaves; pendent clusters 6-12 inches long, not fragrant, showy. Fruit – fall, persisting; large pods, 1-3 seeded.
Texture	Medium.
Color	Foliage – light green. Flower – violet-blue. Fruit – brown.
Culture	Sun. Soil – tolerant; medium drainage; medium fertility. Moisture- medium. Pruning – regularly for restraint. Pest Problems – aphids and scale. Growth Rate – rapid.
Landscape Notes	Aggressive vine valued for flowers and foliage; useful on pergolas and trellises. Difficult to transplant. When planting, restrict roots and fertilize heavily. On small grounds best used trained in tree form. Interesting trunk and stems with age. Most popular and widely planted *Wisteria* species. Rampant growth can girdle trees.
Varieties	'Alba' – white flowers. 'Jako' – extremely fragrant flowers.

SHRUBS 1-4 FEET — EVERGREEN

Azalea (a-zay'lee-a)
   showy shrubs, botanically
   Rhododendrons

hybrida (hy'brid-a)
   hybrid

SATSUKI HYBRID AZALEA

Family Ericaceae

Zones	6, 7, 8.
Size	Height 2-4 feet; spread 2-4 feet.
Form	Compact and spreading. Foliage – alternate, simple, entire, 1-2 inches long. Flower – May to June.
Texture	Fine to medium.
Color	Foliage – dull green. Flower – red, white, orange, pink, purple, or variegated.
Culture	Part shade. Soil – medium to good drainage; medium to high fertility with humus added. Moisture – high. Pruning – remove dead or damaged wood. Pest Problems – lacebug, scale, spider mites, and root rot. Growth Rate – moderate.
Landscape Notes	Large, showy flowers late in season. Most useful for small-scale areas.
Varieties	'Amaghasa' – flowers between deep pink and strong red, 3½ inch diameter, single. Low spreading. 'Beni-kirishima' – flowers orange red, double, 2 inch diameter.

Azalea (a-zay'lee-a)
    showy shrubs, botanically
    Rhododendrons

obtusum (ob-tew'sum)
    blunt or rounded at end

KURUME AZALEA

Family Ericaceae

Zones	6, 7, 8.
Size	Height 2-4 feet; spread 2-5 feet.
Form	Dense and twiggy. Foliage – alternate, simple, entire, ½-1 inch long; shiny. Flower – mid-April; 1-2 inch diameter.
Texture	Medium.
Color	Foliage – dull green. Flower – white, lavender, pink, rose, or bright red.
Culture	Part shade. Soil – good drainage; medium fertility with humus added. Moisture – high. Pruning – remove dead or damaged wood. Pest Problems – lacebugs, scale, spider mites, and root rot. Growth Rate – moderate.
Landscape Notes	Brilliant floral display with best color in light shade. Excellent for small gardens.
Varieties	'Appleblossom' – flowers pink with white throat, single, 1¼ inch diameter. Upright growth. 'Coral Bells' – flowers pink, single, hose-in-hose, 1⅛ inch diameter. Low, spreading growth. 'Delaware Valley White' – flowers white, single, 2 inch diameter.

Berberis (ber'ber-iss)
  Arabic name

verruculosa (vehr-rook-yew-loh'suh)
  warty

WARTY BARBERRY

Family Berberidaceae

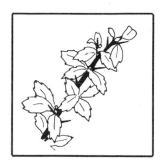

Zones	6, 7.
Size	Height 3-4 feet; spread 3-4 feet.
Form	Compact and rounded with spreading branches. Foliage – alternate, simple, leathery, 1 inch long with spiny edges and margins rolled under. Flower – late April; ½ inch wide. Fruit – fall; ⅓ inch long, berrylike. Twig – thickly warty. Spines – ½ inch long.
Texture	Fine.
Color	Foliage – dark, shining green above, white beneath; winter, bronze, Flower – yellow. Fruit – violet-black.
Culture	Sun to part shade. Soil – tolerant. Moisture – medium. Pruning – remove stray shoots and branches. Pest Problems – none. Growth Rate – slow.
Landscape Notes	Excellent flowering; may be used as specimen plant or as clipped or unclipped hedge for public areas.
Variety	*compacta* – very dwarf variety.

Buxus (bucks'us)
   classical Latin
   for box

harlandii (har-lan'di)
   from proper name

HARLAND BOXWOOD

Family Buxaceae

Zones	7, 8.
Size	Height 2-4 feet; spread 2-3 feet.
Form	Usually broad at top and narrow at base. Foliage – opposite, simple, oblanceolate to oblate, ¾ to 1¼ inches long, somewhat narrowed toward base, notched at tip. Flower – inconspicuous.
Texture	Fine.
Color	Foliage – bright green.
Culture	Sun to part shade. Soil – good drainage; medium fertility. Moisture – medium. Pruning – none. Pest Problems – root rot, nematodes, and spider mites. Growth Rate – moderate.
Landscape Notes	Not good as specimen but excellent in low hedges or as edging plant. Grows well in Coastal Plains. Of refined character, requiring extra care to look best. Untrimmed forms dense and rather top-heavy mound. Space 12 inches for hedge.
Variety	'Richardi' – larger leaves, rapid growth.

Buxus (bucks'us)
    classical Latin
    for box

sempervirens (sem-per-vy'renz)
    evergreen

'Suffruticosa' (suf-frew-ti-ko'sa)
    somewhat shrubby

DWARF BOXWOOD

Family Buxaceae

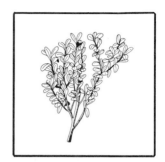

Zones	6,7.
Size	Height 2-3 feet; spread 2-4 feet.
Form	Dense and compact. Assumes globular shape with billowy outline with age. Foliage – opposite, simple, entire, to ¾ inch long. Flower – inconspicuous.
Texture	Fine.
Color	Foliage – dark green.
Culture	Part shade. Soil – good drainage; medium fertility with high organic content. Moisture – medium, Pruning – none. Pest Problems – nematodes, spider mites, leaf miner, root rot, scale, and dogs. Growth Rate – extremely slow.
Landscape Notes	Ideal plant for edging flower beds or garden walks, space 12 inches apart when used for this purpose. Larger plants useful as specimens or accent. Not recommended for Eastern Carolina.

Chamaecyparis (kam-ee-sip'a-ris)
  timber conifers used as
  ornamentals

obtusa (ob-tus'a)
  blunt or rounded at end

'Nana Gracilis' (nay'na; gras'i-lis)
  small, dwarf; graceful, slender

DWARF HINOKI CYPRESS

Family Cupressaceae

Zones	6, 7, 8.
Size	Height 2-4 feet; spread 2-3 feet.
Form	Irregularly twisted and tufted. Central trunk usually leans. Foliage – scalelike, dense, somewhat twisted.
Texture	Medium to fine.
Color	Foliage – deep, shining green.
Culture	Sun to part shade. Soil – tolerant. Moisture – medium to low. Pruning – none. Pest Problems – juniper scale, spruce mites, and bark beetles. Growth Rate – very slow.
Landscape Notes	Excellent as accent or specimen. Not for mass plantings. Loose but formal appearance with interesting character for oriental effects. Frequently sold in nurseries as *C. obtusa* 'Nana.'

Cotoneaster (ko-to'nee-as-ter)
    Greek meaning like quince

horizontalis (hor-ri-zon-tay'lis)
    horizontal

ROCKSPRAY COTONEASTER

Family Rosaceae

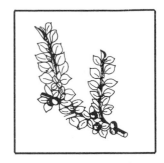

Zones	6, 7, 8.
Size	Height 2-3 feet; spread 5-8 feet.
Form	Low, flat, and very dense with branches spreading almost horizontally, forming flat sprays. Foliage – alternate, simple, entire, ½ inch long, broad elliptic, lustrous and glabrous. Flower – mid-April; small. Fruit – early fall; abundant berries ⅛ inch wide.
Texture	Fine.
Color	Foliage – deep red-green; fall, deep red and orange. Flower – white tinged pink. Fruit – bright red.
Culture	Sun. Soil – tolerant; good drainage; medium fertility. Moisture – low. Pruning – none. Pest Problems – fire blight, scale, spider mites, and lacebug. Growth Rate – slow.
Landscape Notes	Charming plant with long season of handsome foliage and fruits; useful for rock gardens or as ground cover, or draping over low walls. Combines well with stone or wood. Difficult to transplant.

Danae (dan'a-ee)
  named for Pierre Martin
  Dane, writer on plants
  of Piedmont

racemosa (ra-se-mo'sa)
  flowers in racemes

ALEXANDRIAN LAUREL

Family Liliaceae

Zones	7, 8.
Size	Height 3 feet; spread 2-3 feet.
Form	Unbranched stems arching gracefully, somewhat like dwarf bamboo. Foliage – minute, inconspicuous, apparent leaves being alternate flattened stems 3 inches long and ½-1 inch wide. Flower – spring; small in terminal racemes, not showy. Fruit – fall; berry about cherry size.
Texture	Fine to medium.
Color	Foliage – dark green. Flower – white. Fruit – orange-red.
Culture	Shade. Soil – good drainage; high fertility with humus. Moisture – high. Pruning – none. Pest Problems – none. Growth Rate – moderate to slow.
Landscape Notes	May be cut for winter displays. Excellent selection for darker corners of patios and fenced gardens as filler or accent. Unique foliage and fruit.

Daphne (daf'nee)
Greek name for
true laurel

odora (o-do'ra)
fragrant

WINTER DAPHNE

Family Thymelaeaceae

Zones	7, 8.
Size	Height 3-4 feet; spread 3 feet.
Form	Rounded, dense and twiggy. Foliage – alternate, simple, entire, 3 inches long, narrow, oval. Flower – January and February; small, terminal clusters, very fragrant, star-shaped.
Texture	Medium.
Color	Foliage – dark green. Flower – rosy-purple outside, white inside.
Culture	Sun or shade. Soil – good drainage; medium fertility. Moisture – medium. Pruning – none. Pest Problems – fungus diseases. Growth Rate – slow to moderate.
Landscape Notes	Rather expensive and temperamental but beautiful foliage plant for landscape use. Does not respond to fertilization or pruning and is difficult to establish. Most fragrant of all daphnes. Interesting in foreground of mixed shrub plantings, in rock gardens, or as an edging material.
Variety	'Alba' – white flowers.

Euonymus (you-on'i-mus)
   hardy shrubs and vines

fortunei (for-tu'nee-i)
   named for Robert Fortune

'Vegetus' (vej'e-tus)
   vigorous

EVERGREEN BITTERSWEET

Family Celastraceae

Zones	6, 7, 8.
Size	Height 3-4 feet; spread indeterminate.
Form	Irregular and open. Foliage – opposite, entire or serrate, petioled, 2 inches wide. Differs from variety *radicans* principally in orbicular-ovate coarsely toothed leathery leaves and larger flowers and fruits. Fruit – fall; berries.
Texture	Medium.
Color	Foliage – glossy light green. Fruit – orange-red.
Culture	Sun to shade. Soil – tolerant. Moisture – medium to high. Pruning – none or train as vine. Pest Problems – scale and mildew. Growth Rate – moderate.
Landscape Notes	May be used as sheared low hedge, in planter boxes, as climber, or as cover when allowed to trail on ground. Requires spraying to prevent scale infestations. Grown for excellent fruit display and decorative foliage.

Euonymus (you-on'i-mus)
   hardy shrubs and vines

japonicus (ja-pon'i-kus)
   from Japan

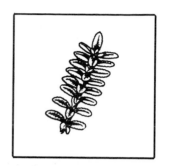

'Microphyllus' (my-kro-fil'lus)
   small-leaved

DWARF JAPANESE EUONYMUS

Family Celastraceae

Zones	7,8.
Size	Height 2-3 feet; spread 18-24 inches.
Form	Upright and rounded. Foliage – alternate, ½-1 inch long. Flower – inconspicuous. Fruit – inconspicuous.
Texture	Medium.
Color	Foliage – glossy, medium green.
Culture	Sun or shade. Soil – medium drainage; medium fertility with high organic content. Moisture – medium to high. Pruning – very little needed except for uniformity in edging use. Pest Problems – scale. Growth Rate – moderate.
Landscape Notes	Frequently used for edging, lawn border, or line definition; twigs break easily. Plant destroyed by Euonymus scale unless regularly sprayed. Easier to propagate and less expensive than boxwood.

Gardenia (gar-de'ni-a)
    named for Alexander Garden
    of Charleston, S.C.

jasminoides (jas-min-oy'deez)
    jasminelike

radicans (rad'i-kanz)
    rooting, especially
    along stem

DWARF GARDENIA

Family Rubiaceae

Zone	8.
Size	Height 1-2 feet; spread 2-2½ feet.
Form	Dwarf with horizontal branching habit. Open and spreading. Foliage – opposite or in 3's, simple, entire, narrow, 2 inches long. Flower – May and June; 2 inches, fragrant.
Texture	Medium to fine.
Color	Foliage – dark lustrous green. Flower – white.
Culture	Sun or part shade. Soil – medium drainage; medium fertility; prefers acid. Moisture – medium. Pruning – none. Pest Problems – white fly and aphids. Growth Rate – moderate to rapid.
Landscape Notes	For Coastal Plain or warmer parts of Piedmont. Excellent in planter boxes. Charming as border or pot plant in sheltered areas.

Hypericum (hy-per'i-kum)
  under, or among heather

patulum (pat'yew-lum)
  spreading

ST.-JOHN'S-WORT

Family Hypericaceae

Zones	6, 7, 8.
Size	Height 3 feet; spread 3 feet.
Form	Spreading with arching branches. Foliage – opposite, simple, entire, 2-3 inches long; semievergreen. Flower – June; 2½ inches wide.
Texture	Medium.
Color	Foliage – dark green above, whitish beneath. Flower – golden yellow.
Culture	Sun. Soil – tolerant. Moisture – low. Pruning – remove dead or old wood. Pest Problems – none. Growth Rate – rapid.
Landscape Notes	More vigorous than species with handsome flower production. Excellent in foreground groupings or in shrub borders and foundation plantings.
Varieties	*grandiflorum* – flowers 3 inches wide. *henryi* – more vigorous than species; larger leaves and flowers. 'Hidcote' – height 2½ feet; spread 2½ feet; fragrant golden yellow flowers. Often cold-damaged. *oblongifolium* – leaves 4 inches long, bluish beneath. 'Sungold' – very hardy; similar to 'Hidcote' in form and flower. *uralum* – leaves 1 inch long; flowers 1 inch wide.

Ilex (eye'lecks)
  hollies

cornuta (kor-new'ta)
  horned

'Rotunda' (roh-tun'da)
  nearly circular

DWARF HORNED HOLLY

Family Aquifoliaceae

Zones	6,7,8.
Size	Height 2-3 feet; spread 3-4 feet.
Form	Compact and rounded. Foliage – alternate, spiny, thick, 3 inches long. Flower – inconspicuous. Fruit – usually none.
Texture	Coarse.
Color	Foliage – glossy light green. Flower – white. Fruit — red.
Culture	Sun or part shade. Soil – tolerant. Moisture – medium. Pruning – none. Pest Problems – scale. Growth Rate – slow.
Landscape Notes	Excellent formal shrub for Piedmont and Coastal Plain. Requires no care when established. May be used as accent or foundation plant, unclipped hedge, or container plant.

Ilex (eye'lecks)
  hollies

crenata (kree-nay'ta)
  scalloped or with
  irregularly waved margin

'Helleri' (hell-er-ri')
  named for Joseph Heller

HELLER JAPANESE HOLLY

Family Aquifoliaceae

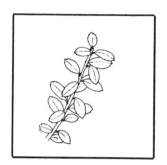

Zones	6, 7.
Size	Height 2-3 feet; spread 3-5 feet.
Form	Spreading, compact and densely twiggy. Foliage – oval, alternate, ½ inch long. Flower – inconspicuous. Fruit – inconspicuous.
Texture	Medium to fine.
Color	Foliage – medium to dark green.
Culture	Sun or shade. Soil – medium drainage; high fertility. Moisture – medium to high. Pruning – none. Pest Problems – scale, spider mites, and nematodes. Growth Rate – slow.
Landscape Notes	Excellent substitute for Dwarf Boxwood. May be used as edging or accent plant. Not recommended for Coastal Plain. Resents droughts and sudden freezes until well-established, 4-6 years.

Ilex (eye'lecks)
hollies

crenata (kree-nay'ta)
scalloped or with
irregularly waved margin

'Kingsville' (kings'vil)
named for Kingsville,
Maryland

KINGSVILLE JAPANESE HOLLY

Family Aquifoliaceae

Zones	6, 7, 8.
Size	Height 3 feet; spread 5-6 feet.
Form	Loose and open mounds. Foliage – alternate, ½-¾ inch long with tip of leaf more pointed and larger than *I. c.* 'Helleri.' Flower – none. Fruit – none.
Texture	Medium to fine.
Color	Foliage – dark green.
Culture	Sun or shade. Soil – medium drainage; high fertility. Moisture – medium. Pruning – none. Pest Problems – scale and nematodes. Growth Rate – slow.
Landscape Notes	Excellent foliage; spreading habit useful for low mass plantings. Tolerant of city conditions. Considered superior to Heller Holly in color and form.

Ilex (eye'lecks)
　　hollies

crenata (kree-nay'ta)
　　scalloped or with irregularly
　　waved margin

'Kingsville Green Cushion' (kings'vil)
　　named for Kingsville, Maryland

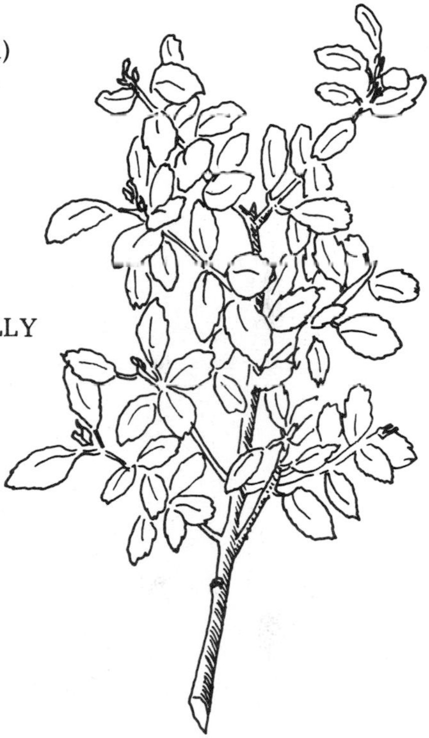

KINGSVILLE GREEN CUSHION HOLLY

Family Aquifoliaceae

Zones	6,7,8.
Size	Height 10-18 inches; spread 2½-3 feet.
Form	Very dwarf and spreading, solid foliage mass. Foliage – alternate, ½ inch long, similar to *I.c.* 'Helleri'. Flower – none. Fruit – none.
Texture	Fine.
Color	Foliage – dark green.
Culture	Sun or shade. Soil – medium drainage; high fertility. Moisture – medium. Pruning – none. Pest Problems – scale and nematodes. Growth Rate – slow.
Landscape Notes	Good foliage. Excellent for low mass planting; spreading habit of growth.

Ilex (eye'lecks)
  hollies

crenata (kre-nay'ta)
  scalloped or with
  irregularly waved
  margin

'Repandens' (ree-pan'denz)
  wavy-margined

REPANDEN JAPANESE HOLLY

Family Aquifoliaceae

Zones	6, 7, 8.
Size	Height 1-3 feet; spread 5-6 feet.
Form	Spreading and dense. Foliage – alternate, ½-1 inch long. Flower – inconspicuous. Fruit – inconspicuous.
Texture	Medium to fine.
Color	Foliage – olive green.
Culture	Sun or shade. Soil – medium drainage; high fertility. Moisture – medium. Pruning – none. Pest Problems – scale and nematodes. Growth Rate – slow.
Landscape Notes	Selected for foliage color and low, compact growth. Good substitute for Dwarf Boxwood.

Ilex (eye'lecks)
   hollies

crenata (kree-nay'ta)
   scalloped or with
   irregularly waved margin

'Stokes' (stoks)
   unexplained

STOKES JAPANESE HOLLY

Family Aquifoliaceae

Zones	6, 7, 8.
Size	Height 1-3 feet; spread 3-4 feet.
Form	Spreading, compact, and densely twiggy. Foliage – alternate, ¼ - ½ inch long; tip more rounded than *I. c.* 'Helleri'. Flower – inconspicuous. Fruit – inconspicuous.
Texture	Fine to medium.
Color	Foliage – medium to dark green.
Culture	Sun or shade. Soil – medium drainage; high fertility. Moisture – medium. Pruning – none. Pest Problems – spider mites, scale, and nematodes. Growth Rate – slow.
Landscape Notes	Less globose in form than *I. c.* 'Helleri'. Excellent as specimen, edging, or accent plant. Does well in city gardens. Considered superior to Heller Holly in color and form.

Ilex (eye'lecks)
   hollies

vomitoria (vom-i-tor'i-a)
   emetic

'Nana' (nay'na)
   small, dwarf

DWARF YAUPON

Family Aquifoliaceae

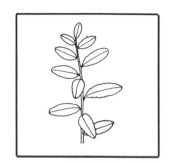

Zones	7, 8.
Size	Height 2-4 feet; spread 3-5 feet.
Form	Symmetrical and dense. Foliage – alternate, to 1 inch long. Flower – none. Fruit – none.
Texture	Fine.
Color	Foliage – gray-green. Bark – gray.
Culture	Sun or shade. Soil – medium drainage; medium fertility. Moisture – medium. Pruning – none. Pest Problems – none. Growth Rate – slow to moderate.
Landscape Notes	Excellent as low edging, specimen, or accent plant. Rather formal in character. Withstands drought when well-established. Useful as low growing foundation plant. Particularly valuable for Coastal Plains.

Lavandula (la-van'dew-la)
  Latin to wash, in allusion
  to use in bath water

officinalis (of-fish-i-na'lis)
  medicinal

ENGLISH LAVENDER

Family Labiatae

Zones	6, 7, 8.
Size	Height 2½-3½ feet; spread 3-4 feet.
Form	Irregular to semiglobe with vertical stem growth, medium to very dense. Foliage – opposite, fuzzy, aromatic, 1 inch long and ⅛ inch wide. Flower – May and June; fragrant small spikes 2 inches long on stems 4-8 inches long above foliage.
Texture	Medium to fine.
Color	Foliage – gray-green. Flower – lavender.
Culture	Sun. Soil – good drainage; medium fertility; prefers neutral to alkaline. Moisture – medium to low. Pruning – none. Pest Problems – none. Growth Rate -moderate.
Landscape Notes	Noted for fragrant leaves and flowers; dry seed heads very fragrant when crushed. Essential in herb gardens and may be clipped to form low hedge or border. Space 2 feet apart as hedging.
Variety	'Hidcote' – dwarf and more compact.

Leucothoe (lew-ko'tho-ee)
   shrubs of heath family

axillaris (ak-si-ler'is)
   axil-flowering

COASTAL LEUCOTHOE

Family Ericaceae

Zones	6, 7, 8.
Size	Height 3-4 feet; spread to 4 feet.
Form	Graceful and informal with arching branches. Foliage – alternate, 3-5 inches long, finely toothed. Flower – April; bell-shaped on racemes in axils of leaves.
Texture	Medium.
Color	Foliage – dark green; winter, purple-green. Flower – white or pinkish-white.
Culture	Part shade or shade. Soil – medium drainage; medium fertility; prefers acid woodland conditions. Moisture – high with high humidity. Pruning – remove 2 and 3 year old canes after bloom to stimulate new growth. Pest Problems – none. Growth Rate – slow until established.
Landscape Notes	Excellent in masses. Arching habit contrasts with more upright shade plants such as rhododendrons. Good selection for enclosed city gardens or naturalized along stream banks and woodland trails. Mulch heavily.

Leucothoe (lew-ko'tho-ee)
shrubs of heath family

fontanesiana (fon-ta-nee'zi-a-na)
named for R.L. Desfontaines,
French botanist

DROOPING LEUCOTHOE

Family Ericaceae

Zones	6, 7, 8.
Size	Height 3-4 feet; spread 4-6 feet.
Form	Graceful with long arching branches. Spreads by underground stems. Foliage – alternate, 3-5 inches long, leathery, lanceolate. Flower – late April; ¼ inch in 2-3 inch sprays or loose axillary racemes drooping below branches, waxy, fragrant. Fruit – fall; 5-lobed capsules.
Texture	Medium to coarse.
Color	Foliage – rich, lustrous dark green; winter, bronze-purple. Flower-white. Fruit-green turning brown. Bark – reddish.
Culture	Part shade or shade. Soil – medium drainage; medium fertility; prefers acid loam. Moisture – high. Pruning – remove 2 and 3 year old canes after blooming to stimulate new growth. Pest Problems – none. Growth Rate – slow.
Landscape Notes	Good color and habit; useful for massing and as undergrowth for naturalizing in woods. Good filler between other shrubs. Easy to transplant. Interesting in enclosed small city gardens. Requires heavy mulching. Formerly known as *L. catesbaei*.
Variety	'Nana' – dwarf form; height 2 feet, spread 3 feet.

Ligustrum (ly-gus'trum)
classical Latin name
of privet

japonicum (ja-pon'i-kum)
from Japan

'Rotundifolium' (ro-tun-di-fo'li-um)
round-leaved

CURLYLEAF LIGUSTRUM

Family Oleaceae

Zones	7, 8.
Size	Height to 4 feet; spread 3 feet.
Form	Upright and columnar, dense. Foliage – opposite, thick, curved, 1-2½ inches long, crowded on short branches. Flower – inconspicuous panicles. Fruit – berrylike.
Texture	Medium.
Color	Foliage – glossy dark green. Flower – white. Fruit – black.
Culture	Sun or part shade. Soil – tolerant; medium drainage; medium fertility. Moisture – medium. Pruning – none. Pest Problems – white fly. Growth Rate – slow.
Landscape Notes	Useful as container specimen. Interesting twisted habit of leaf growth. Withstands adverse city conditions and drought fairly well. Also listed as *L. coriaceum*.

Lonicera (lon-iss'er-ra)
honeysuckles

yunnanensis (yun-a-nen'sis)
from Yunnan, China

YUNNAN HONEYSUCKLE

Family Caprifoliaceae

Zones	7, 8.
Size	Height 2-3 feet; spread 3-4 feet.
Form	Low, creeping, arching, or twining. Foliage – opposite, 1 inch long. Flower – spring; 1 inch long.
Texture	Fine.
Color	Foliage – medium green. Flower – yellow.
Culture	Sun. Soil – good drainage; medium fertility. Moisture – medium to low. Pruning – none. Pest Problems – none. Growth Rate – moderate.
Landscape Notes	Useful as ground cover or in rock gardens. Good for quick and temporary effect.

Mahonia (ma-ho'ni-a)
   named for M'Mahon,
   American horticulturist

aquifolium (a-kwi-fo'li-um)
   holly-leaved

OREGON HOLLY-GRAPE

Family Berberidaceae

Zones	6, 7.
Size	Height 3-4 feet; spread 3-5 feet.
Form	Informal, irregular, becoming broadly clumped; upright stems with few branches. Foliage – alternate, leathery, compound, with 5-9 spiny hollylike leaflets. Flower – late March to May; erect terminal clusters 3 inches long, fragrant. Fruit – early summer; grapelike clusters.
Texture	Coarse.
Color	Foliage – glossy dark green; fall and winter, reddish purple to bronze. Flower – yellow. Fruit – blue-black.
Culture	Part shade to shade. Soil – medium drainage; medium fertility. Moisture – medium. Pruning – remove 2-3 year old canes to stimulate new growth. Pest Problems – leaf miner and lacebug. Growth Rate – fairly slow.
Landscape Notes	Valued for foliage and flowers. Excellent for foundation plantings in part shade or for shrub borders. Avoid placing near red brick buildings. Not recommended for Coastal Plains. Withstands exposure to wind. Spreads slowly.
Varieties	'Compactum' – very glossy dark green leaves becoming bronze in in winter. Height 1-2 feet. 'Golden Abundance' – vigorous grower with profuse dense golden yellow flower clusters.

Pinus (py'nus)
old Latin name
for pine

mugo (mew'go)
native name in Alps
for Swiss mountain
pine

'Compacta' (kom-pack'ta)
compact, dense

MUGO PINE

Family Pinaceae

Zones	6, 7, 8.
Size	Height 3-4 feet; spread 2-4 feet.
Form	Compact and globe-shaped. Foliage – needles in clusters of 2, 2 inches long and crowded. Attractive candlelike new growth in spring.
Texture	Fine.
Color	Foliage – deep green.
Culture	Sun. Soil – good drainage; medium to low fertility. Moisture – medium. Pruning – remove candles to create density. Pest Problems – pine root rot and scale. Growth Rate – slow.
Landscape Notes	Varies greatly from seed, some plants reaching a height of 8 feet. Use only grafted plants for dwarf forms. Excellent planted in informal masses exposed to full sun and wind. Useful as specimen. Excellent container plant.

Raphiolepis (raf-i-oll'ep-is)
 Greek needle scale,
 referring to bracts
 in inflorescence

indica (in'di-ka)
 from India

INDIA HAWTHORN

Family Rosaceae

Zones	7,8.
Size	Height 3-4 feet; spread 4-5 feet.
Form	Spreading, open, irregularly branched. Foliage – alternate, thick and leathery, pointed with margins serrated, 1½-2½ inches long. Flower – April; terminal panicles. Fruit – fall; small berries, ½ inch diameter.
Texture	Medium to coarse.
Color	Foliage – dark green; winter, purplish if exposed. Flower – white or pink. Fruit – black.
Culture	Sun or shade. Soil – tolerant; medium drainage; medium fertility; prefers slightly alkaline. Moisture – medium. Pruning – none. Pest Problems – nematodes, scale, and blight. Growth Rate – slow.
Landscape Notes	Strong in character with dramatic appearance. Good informal hedge with excellent foliage and flower color combination. Ideal for coastal regions and warmer parts of Piedmont. Tolerates wind and salt spray.
Varieties	'Enchantress' – large flower clusters, large leaves; round form. 'Fascination' – flower rose with white center, starlike in appearance.

Rosmarinus (ros-ma-ry'nus)
  rosemary

officinalis (of-fish-i-na'lis)
  medicinal

ROSEMARY

Family Labiatae

Zones	6, 7, 8.
Size	Height 2-4 feet; spread 2 feet.
Form	Irregular and loose with upright stems. Foliage – opposite, entire, narrow, to 1 inch long, aromatic. Flower – fall, winter and early spring; inconspicuous spikes.
Texture	Fine.
Color	Foliage – green to gray-green. Flower – pale violet-blue.
Culture	Sun. Soil – good drainage; low fertility. Moisture – low. Pruning – none, or as needed to maintain shape. Pest Problems – none. Growth Rate – slow until established.
Landscape Notes	For herb gardens and as accent or background for flowers. May be used as low hedge in warm areas with careful pruning.
Variety	'Prostratus' – trailing ground cover for zone 8.

Skimmia (skim'i-a)
    from skimmi, Japanese
    word signifying harmful
    fruit

japonica (ja-pon'i-ca)
    from Japan

JAPANESE SKIMMIA

Family Rutaceae

Zones	7,8.
Size	Height 4 feet; spread to 3 feet.
Form	Loose, rounded, moundlike. Foliage – alternate, simple, 3-5 inches long, 1½ inches wide. Flower – April; small in large terminal panicles, fragrant, sexes separate. Fruit – fall and winter; berry, ⅓ inch diameter in large clustered heads.
Texture	Coarse.
Color	Foliage – dark green. Flower – white. Fruit – scarlet.
Culture	Part shade or shade. Soil – good drainage; medium fertility with humus added. Moisture – low to medium. Pruning – remove cold damaged stems and dried berry stalks. Pest Problems – none. Growth Rate – slow.
Landscape Notes	Grown for excellent foliage, flowers, and fruit. Flowers on male plants larger and more fragrant. Useful in foundation plantings and foreground of mixed shrub plantings or in planter boxes.

Skimmia (skim'i-a)
  from skimmi, Japanese word
  signifying harmful fruit

reevesiana (reevs'ee-an-na)
  named for R. G. Reeves of Texas

REEVES SKIMMIA

Family Rutaceae

Zones	7, 8.
Size	Height 1½-2 feet; spread 2-3 feet.
Form	Loose but more compact than *S. japonica*. Foliage – alternate, simple, 4 inches long. Flower – April; perfect, ½ inch long. Fruit – fall and winter; berry ½ inch thick.
Texture	Medium to coarse.
Color	Foliage – dark flat green. Flower – white. Fruit – red.
Culture	Part shade. Soil – good drainage; medium fertility with acid humus added. Moisture – high. Pruning – remove cold damaged stems and dried berry stalks. Pest Problems – none. Growth Rate – slow.
Landscape Notes	Grown for foliage, flowers, and fruits. Excellent for small gardens.

Viburnum (vy-bur'num)
    classical Latin name
    of wayfaring tree

davidii (da-vid'i)
    from proper name

DAVID VIBURNUM

Family Caprifoliaceae

Zones	7,8.
Size	Height 3 feet; spread 3-5 feet.
Form	Rounded, compact mound of medium density. Foliage – opposite, leathery, to 5½ inches long, slightly toothed at edges and deeply veined. Flower – early summer; clusters 2-3 inches wide. Fruit – early fall; berrylike.
Texture	Medium to coarse.
Color	Foliage – dark green. Flower – white. Fruit – light blue.
Culture	Sun or part shade. Soil – tolerant; medium drainage; medium fertility. Moisture – medium. Pruning – none. Pest Problems – none. Growth Rate – moderate.
Landscape Notes	Excellent low-growing foundation plant. Of dignified and rather formal character. Plant both male and female forms to obtain fruit.

Yucca (yuk'ka)
Latinized version of
Spanish vernacular for
some other desert plant

filamentosa (fill-a-men-to'sa)
threadlike

ADAM'S NEEDLE YUCCA

Family Liliaceae

Zones	6, 7, 8.
Size	Height 1½-4 feet; spread 2½-4 feet.
Form	Fairly open. Foliage – stiff blades 2½ feet long, upright and outward from central crown, produces side shoots. Flower – late spring and summer; bell-shaped 2-3 inches wide on central stalk 3-5 feet high. Fruit – September and October; capsules 2 inches long.
Texture	Coarse.
Color	Foliage – medium green. Flower – greenish-white. Fruit – green to brown.
Culture	Sun or part shade. Soil – medium to good drainage; low fertility. Moisture – low. Pruning – annual removal of old flower stalks and unsightly foliage. Pest Problems – leaf spot or blight during rainy growing season. Growth Rate – moderate.
Landscape Notes	Very resistant to drought and adverse growing conditions. Hazardous near play areas because of sharp, pointed leaf blades. Very stiff visual effect; contrasts in texture and form with surrounding plant materials. Available in variegated leaf form. Also called *Y. smalliana*.
Variety	*concava* – spoonlike leaves which are broad and stiff.

SHRUBS 1-4 FEET — DECIDUOUS

Chaenomeles (kee-nom'e-lees)
   Greek meaning split apple

japonica (ja-pon'i-ka)
   from Japan

JAPANESE FLOWERING
QUINCE

Family Rosaceae

Zones	6, 7, 8.
Size	Height 2-3 feet; spread 2-3 feet.
Form	Open and spreading. Foliage – alternate, simple, long, coarsely toothed, based wedge-shaped. Flower – early spring; single, 1¼ inch diameter. Fruit – autumn; resembling miniature apples 1½ inches wide, fragrant, edible. Stem – thorny.
Texture	Medium.
Color	Foliage – medium green. Flower – red to light orange. Fruit – yellow.
Culture	Sun or part shade. Soil – very tolerant; medium drainage; low to medium fertility. Moisture – medium. Pruning – remove leggy, non-flowering shoots. Pest Problems – scale, fire blight, and aphids. Growth Rate – fairly rapid.
Landscape Notes	Withstands city conditions very well. Valued for showy flowers. Needs leafy background. Excellent for floral arrangements. Oriental in character.
Varieties	*alpina* – dense growth, height 1 foot, orange flowers. 'Minerva' – velvety cherry red flowers; large and spreading growth.

Deutzia (doot'zi-a)
    named for Johan van
    der Deutz

gracilis (gras'i-lis)
    graceful, slender

SLENDER DEUTZIA

Family Saxifragaceae

Zones	6, 7, 8.
Size	Height 3-4 feet; spread to 4 feet.
Form	Graceful, rounded, and compact. Branches slender and arching. Foliage – opposite, simple, toothed, 2½ inches long. Flower – late April, on wood of previous season; single, ¾ inch wide in 2-4 inch upright clusters.
Texture	Medium to fine.
Color	Foliage – neutral, pale green. Flower – white.
Culture	Sun or part shade. Soil – tolerant; good drainage; low to medium fertility. Moisture – low to medium. Pruning – remove old stems annually after flowering. Pest Problems – none. Growth Rate – slow.
Landscape Notes	Excellent as filler in mixed shrub borders and flower gardens, or as low hedge around entrance, patio, or walk. Useful for small gardens or foundation plantings. Will tolerate neglect. Lacks vigor in warmer areas of Coastal Plain. Relatively neutral after flowering.

Hydrangea (hy-dran'jee-a)
  hardy shrubs, vines

arborescens (ar-bore-ress'ens)
  almost treelike

'Grandiflora' (grand-di-flo'ra)
  large or showy flowered

SNOWHILL HYDRANGEA

Family Saxifragaceae

Zones	6, 7.
Size	Height 3 feet; spread 3-5 feet.
Form	Upright, open and loose mounds with many branches suckering. Foliage – opposite, simple, toothed, oval, 3-6 inches long. Flower – June and July; rounded heads, 6 inch diameter; florets sterile.
Texture	Coarse.
Color	Foliage – light green. Flower – white turning green.
Culture	Sun or part shade. Soil – good drainage; medium to high fertility. Moisture – medium. Pruning – cut back annually in late winter to encourage vigorous new growth. Pest Problems – none. Growth Rate – rapid.
Landscape Notes	Best planted in generous drifts. Easy to grow and very hardy. Grown for summer flowers. Useful in foreground of shrub borders. Not recommended for Coastal Plain.

Hypericum (hy-per'i-kum)
under or among heather

kalmianum (kal-mee-ay'num)
named for Peter Kalm
of Sweden

KALM ST.-JOHN'S-WORT

Family Hypericaceae

Zones	6, 7, 8.
Size	Height 3 feet; spread 3 feet.
Form	Rounded and loose. Foliage – opposite, 1-2½ inches long, ½ inch wide. Flower – early July; single, 1 inch diameter, cup-shaped, somewhat fragrant. Stem – 4-angled with peeling bark.
Texture	Fine.
Color	Foliage – blue-green above, whitish beneath. Flower – waxy, bright yellow.
Culture	Sun. Soil – tolerant. Moisture – low. Pruning – flowers produced on wood of current season, remove old wood in early spring. Pest problems – none. Growth Rate – rapid.
Landscape Notes	Handsome summer flowers enhance value as edging for shrub border or foundation plantings. May be used to form low hedge along walks, drives, walls, or fences. Often evergreen in warmer areas.

Hypericum (hy-per'i-kum)
under or among heather

moserianum (mo-ze-ri'num)
named for Moser of
Versailles

GOLDFLOWER

Family Hypericaceae

Zones	6, 7.
Size	Height 2-3 feet; spread 3 feet or more.
Form	Loose and rounded with arching stems, broader than tall. Foliage – opposite, 2 inches long. Flower – July and August; cup-shaped, single, 2 inch diameter; odorless. Fruit – fall, persisting through winter; capsules. Bark – peeling.
Texture	Medium to fine.
Color	Foliage – gray-green. Flower – yellow.
Culture	Sun. Soil – tolerant. Moisture – medium to high. Pruning – early spring; thin occasionally. Pest Problems – none. Growth Rate – fairly rapid.
Landscape Notes	Will thrive under poor growing conditions. Interesting small shrub valued for summer bloom; excellent for cover planting, facer shrub, or as undergrowth; may be used in rock gardens and in perennial borders. Not recommended for Coastal Plain.

Jasminum (jas'min-um)
  Arabic name for
  jasmine

nudiflorum (new-di-flo'rum)
  flowers without leaves

WINTER JASMINE

Family Oleaceae

Zones	6, 7, 8.
Size	Height 2-4 feet; spread 3-5 feet.
Form	Low spreading with pendulous 4-angled branches. Foliage – opposite, trifoliate leaflets 1 inch long. Flower – February; 1 inch diameter. Fruit – small berry.
Texture	Medium.
Color	Foliage – glossy green. Flower – yellow. Fruit – black. Stem – green.
Culture	Sun or shade. Soil – tolerant; medium drainage; low fertility. Moisture – medium. Pruning – heavy thinning every 3-4 years for rejuvenation. Pest Problems – spider mites. Growth Rate – moderate.
Landscape Notes	Twig tips root easily in contact with cultivated soil. Suitable for covering banks. Will survive in poor soil. Good for irregular, loose hedges. Attractive winter bloom. Little care required.

Potentilla (po-ten-till'a)
diminutive from *potens*,
powerful; alluding to
reputed medicinal power

fruticosa (fro-ti-ko'sa)
shrubby

BUSH CINQUEFOIL

Family Rosaceae

Zones	6, 7, 8.
Size	Height 2-4 feet; spread 3-5 feet.
Form	Rounded and billowing, stems upright and much branched, dense. Foliage – alternate, pinnately compound with 3-7 leaflets ½-1½ inches long. Flower – mid-April and continuing all summer; single, ¾ inch diameter. Fruit – capsule.
Texture	Fine.
Color	Foliage – medium green above, whitish beneath. Flower – yellow or white. Fruit – brown.
Culture	Sun or part shade. Soil – tolerant; good drainage. Moisture – medium. Pruning – trim lightly in fall to remove dried fruit. Pest Problems – none. Growth Rate – moderate.
Landscape Notes	Valued for long flowering season. Excellent in rock gardens, over stone walls, or as ground cover. Interesting informal hedge or edging material.

SHRUBS 4-6 FEET — EVERGREEN

Abelia (a-bee'li-a)
   named for Abel,
   physician and author

grandiflora (gran-di-flo'ra)
   large or showy flowered

GLOSSY ABELIA

Family Caprifoliaceae

Zones	6, 7, 8.
Size	Height 4-6 feet; spread 3-5 feet.
Form	Semiglobal; many canes from ground level; fairly open to medium density. Foliage – opposite, to 1½ inches long, glossy. Flower – summer; ¾ inch in clusters of 1-4.
Texture	Medium to fine.
Color	Foliage – purplish-green; winter, bronze-purple. Flower-pinkish-white with reddish bracts.
Culture	Sun or shade. Soil – medium to good drainage; medium fertility with high organic content. Moisture – medium. Pruning – pinch new growth tips in spring for compactness; occasional thinning needed. Pest Problems – aphids. Growth Rate – moderate. .
Landscape Notes	Good plant for medium height informal hedges or for background. Less expensive than most evergreens. Iron chlorosis common; not well adapted to deep sandy soils. Leaf drop from low temperatures, lack of pruning, and starvation.
Varieties	'Prostrata' – white flowers; used as ground cover. 'Sherwood' – excellent 2-3 feet trailing form.

Aucuba (aw-kew'ba)
  Latinized from
  Japanese name

japonica (ja-pon'i-ka)
  from Japan

JAPANESE AUCUBA

Family Cornaceae

Zones	7,8.
Size	Height 4-5 feet; spread 3-4 feet.
Form	Irregular with medium density. Foliage – opposite, 4-8 inches long. Flower – March; inconspicuous panicles 2-5 inches long. Fruit – winter; berries. Dioecious, plant both sexes to ensure fruiting.
Texture	Coarse.
Color	Foliage – deep green. Flower – brownish-white. Fruit – red.
Culture	Shade; sun causes burning of leaves. Soil – medium drainage; high fertility; prefers heavy soils. Moisture – medium to high. Pruning – keep plant low and compact. Pest Problems – spider mites and scale. Growth Rate – slow to moderate.
Landscape Notes	Excellent for dark corners or shady locations. May be grown in planter boxes. Foliage useful in flower arrangements.
Varieties	'Nana' – dwarf form, about 2 feet in height. *variegata* – leaves marked with yellow spots. Use in moderation. Golddust Tree.

Azalea (a-zay'lee-a)
 showy shrubs, botanically
 Rhododendrons

hybrida (hy'brid-a)
 hybrid

GLENN DALE AZALEA

Family Ericaceae

Zones	6, 7, 8.
Size	Height 4-6 feet; spread 3-4 feet.
Form	Upright or spreading depending on variety. Foliage – alternate, simple, entire, 1-2 inches long. Flower – mid-April to May; 2-4 inches wide.
Texture	Medium.
Color	Foliage – dark green to medium green. Flower – white, rose, purple, salmon, red, or pink.
Culture	Part shade. Soil – medium drainage; medium fertility with high organic content. Moisture – high. Pruning – none. Pest Problems – lacebug, scale, spider mites, and root rot. Growth Rate – moderate.
Landscape Notes	Brilliant floral display with different varieties covering entire azalea blooming season. Somewhat more cold hardy than Kurume azalea.
Varieties	'Aphrodite' – flowers rose-pink, single, 2 inch diameter. Upright growth with spreading branches. 'Copperman' – flowers deep brick-red, single, 2¾-3 inch diameter. Dense, spreading.

Azalea (a-zay'lee-a)
   showy shrubs, botanically
   Rhododendrons

obtusum (ob-tew'sum)
   blunt or rounded at end

kaempferi (kamp'fer-i)
   named for Engelbert
   Kaempfer

KAEMPFERI AZALEA

Family Ericaceae

Zones	6,7,8.
Size	Height 4-6 feet; spread 4-6 feet.
Form	Upright and open. Foliage – alternate, simple, entire, pubescent, 1-2 inches long. Flower – late April and early May; 1½ - 2½ inches wide, single or hose-in-hose.
Texture	Medium.
Color	Foliage – medium green. Flower – red, pink, purple, or white.
Culture	Part shade. Soil – medium drainage; medium fertility with high organic content. Moisture – high. Pruning – none. Pest Problems -- lacebug, scale, spider mites, and root rot. Growth Rate – moderate.
Landscape Notes	Blooms late enough to escape frosts. Excellent for woodland plantings, especially under pines. Somewhat deciduous. Easier to grow and less demanding than Kurume azaleas.

Berberis (ber'ber-iss)
Arabic name

julianae (jew-li-a'na)
named for
Mrs. C.K. Schneider

WINTERGREEN BARBERRY
Family Berberidaceae

Zones	6, 7, 8.
Size	Height 4-6 feet; spread 2-5 feet.
Form	Dense and rounded with stiff thorns to 1½ inches long. Foliage – alternate in rosettes, sharply toothed, narrow-elliptic, 3 inches long. Flower – early April; ½ inch wide in clusters. Fruit – late fall; ovoid-oblong berries.
Texture	Fine to medium.
Color	Foliage – glossy deep green. Flower – yellow. Fruit – bluish-black. Bark – yellowish to brown.
Culture	Sun or part shade. Soil – very tolerant; medium drainage; medium fertility. Moisture – medium. Pruning – none. Pest Problems – none. Growth Rate – slow.
Landscape Notes	Very handsome shrub. Good as background material. May be used as specimen, hedge, border, or background material. Impenetrable because of thorns. Combines well with broadleaf evergreens.

Buxus (bucks'us)
  classical Latin
  for box

microphylla (my-kro-fil'la)
  small-leaved

japonica (ja-pon'i-ka)
  from Japan

JAPANESE BOXWOOD

Family Buxaceae

Zones	7, 8.
Size	Height 4-5 feet; spread 3-4 feet.
Form	Grows upright for first few years and then forms flattened globe. Foliage – opposite, simple, entire, 1¼ inches long. Flower – inconspicuous.
Texture	Medium.
Color	Foliage – glossy yellowish-green. Flower – white to green.
Culture	Sun or shade. Soil – good drainage; medium fertility. Moisture – medium. Pruning – needs frequent clipping to retain compactness in shade or part shade. Pest Problems – boxwood leaf miner, spider mites, and nematodes. Growth Rate – moderate.
Landscape Notes	Larger leaves than species. Excellent sheared or natural hedge. Good low specimen plant. Not as fast-growing as *B. sempervirens*, but better adapted to Coastal Plain areas. Not hardy in mountain area.

Buxus (buck'us)
   classical Latin
   for box

sempervirens (sem-per-vy'renz)
   evergreen

AMERICAN BOXWOOD

Family Buxaceae

Zones	6, 7.
Size	Height 3-5 feet; spread 3-4 feet.
Form	Upright globe with many canes from crown; very dense. Foliage – opposite, simple, entire, pointed, to 1¼ inches long. Flower – inconspicuous. Fruit – inconspicuous.
Texture	Fine to medium.
Color	Foliage – lustrous dark green.
Culture	Part shade to shade. Soil – good drainage; medium fertility with high organic content. Moisture – medium. Pruning – occasional light shearing for compactness. Pest Problems – nematodes, boxwood leaf miner, spider mites, root rot, and dogs. Growth Rate – moderate to rapid.
Landscape Notes	Most dignified of shrubs lending elegance to any situation. Does well in cool sections of Piedmont.

Euonymus (you-on'i-mus)
  hardy shrubs and vines

kiautschovicus (ky-cho'va-kus)
  unexplained

SPREADING EUONYMUS

Family Celastraceae

Zones	6, 7, 8.
Size	Height 4-6 feet; spread 4-6 feet.
Form	Informal and open with broad spread. Foliage – opposite, simple, thin, bluntly fine-toothed, 2-6 inches long. Flower – August; negligible size but very numerous, giving attractive filmy appearance. Fruit – fall; ½ inch diameter.
Texture	Medium to coarse.
Color	Foliage – bright green. Flower – greenish-white. Fruit – orange.
Culture	Sun or shade. Soil – very tolerant; medium drainage; medium fertility. Moisture – medium. Pruning – none. Pest Problems – scale. Growth Rate – rapid.
Landscape Notes	May be trained as vine on walls or fences; climbs by aerial roots. Lower branches sometimes prostrate and rooting. Useful as hedge, screen, border, or foundation planting. Not as susceptible to scale as some other *Euonymus* species. Often listed as *E. patens*.

Fatsia (fat'si-a)
   derived from
   Japanese vernacular
   for plant

japonica (ja-pon'i-ka)
   from Japan

JAPANESE FATSIA

Family Araliaceae

Zones	7, 8.
Size	Height 4-6 feet; spread 4-6 feet.
Form	Rather globular and open. Foliage – alternate, leathery, 7-9 lobes, 8-12 inch diameter. Flower – fall; round heads 1-2 inches wide. Fruit – winter; berries ¼ inch diameter.
Texture	Coarse.
Color	Foliage – glossy dark green. Flower – white. Fruit – light blue.
Culture	Shade. Soil – tolerant; medium drainage; medium fertility. Moisture – medium. Pruning – remove older stems to maintain desired size. Pest Problems – none. Growth Rate – moderate.
Landscape Notes	Most useful for warmer parts of Piedmont and Coastal Plain. Prefers protected spot in deep shade. Excellent espaliered or in planter boxes; very tolerant of confined city conditions. Tropical in appearance. Tolerates salt spray. Ideal specimen for patios.

Gardenia (gar-de'ni-a)
   named for Alexander
   Garden of Charleston,
   South Carolina

jasminoides (jas-min-oy'deez)
   jasminelike

CAPE-JASMINE

Family Rubiaceae

Zone	8.
Size	Height 4-6 feet; spread 4-5 feet.
Form	Rounded and open. Foliage – opposite or whorled in 2's or 3's, to 4 inches long. Flower – May and June; waxy, to 3 inches wide, fragrant.
Texture	Medium.
Color	Foliage – lustrous dark green. Flower – white.
Culture	Sun or part shade. Soil – medium drainage; medium to high fertility with iron added. Moisture – medium. Pruning – none. Pest Problems – white fly, mealybug, sooty mold, and nematodes. Growth Rate – moderate.
Landscape Notes	Should be used as specimen shrub; requires careful maintenance. Several forms with single or double flowers. Protect roots carefully during transplanting. Not cold hardy in mountain area.
Variety	*fortuniana* – large flowers to 4 inches wide, double and camellia-like; larger leaves than species.

Ilex (eye'lecks)
    hollies

crenata (kree-nay'ta)
    scalloped or with
    irregularly waved margin

'Convexa' (kon-vex'a)
    small, convex

CONVEXA JAPANESE HOLLY

Family Aquifoliaceae

Zones	6, 7, 8.
Size	Height 4-6 feet; spread 3-5 feet.
Form	Rounded, somewhat stiff and strawlike. Foliage – alternate, ½ inch long, oval, cupped and crowded on stems. Flower – inconspicuous. Fruit – fall; berries ¼ inch diameter.
Texture	Fine to medium.
Color	Foliage – glossy black-green. Fruit – dull black.
Culture	Sun or shade; part shade best in Coastal Plain. Soil – medium drainage; medium fertility with nitrogen added. Moisture – medium. Pruning – snip back new branches in early summer to maintain compactness. Pest Problems – spider mites, usually scale-resistant. Growth Rate – moderate.
Landscape Notes	Useful broad-leaved evergreen, growing well throughout Southeast. Fine as foundation plant or in masses. Good substitute for boxwoods and may be developed into formal or informal hedge.

Ilex (eye'lecks)
  hollies

crenata (kree-nay'ta)
  scalloped or with
  irregularly waved margin

'Hetzi' (het-sy')
  from proper
  name

HETZI JAPANESE HOLLY

Family Aquifoliaceae

Zones	6, 7, 8.
Size	Height 4-6 feet; spread 5-7 feet.
Form	Spreading and rounded. Foliage – alternate, ¾ inch long, cupped. Flower – inconspicuous. Fruit – fall; berries ¼ inch diameter.
Texture	Medium to fine.
Color	Foliage – medium green. Fruit – black.
Culture	Sun or shade. Soil – medium drainage; medium fertility with high organic content. Moisture – medium. Pruning – maintain size. Pest Problems – scale, spider mites, and nematodes. Growth Rate – moderate.
Landscape Notes	Similar to *I.c.* 'Convexa' except in color. Vigorous, spreading habit of growth. Good background for azaleas. Needs part shade in Coastal Plain areas.

Ilex (eye'lecks)
   hollies

crenata (kree-nay'ta)
   scalloped or with
   irregularly waved margin

'Microphylla' (my-kro-fill'la)
   small-leaved

LITTLELEAF
JAPANESE HOLLY

Family Aquifoliaceae

Zones	6, 7, 8.
Size	Height 4-6 feet; spread 5-7 feet.
Form	Low but somewhat upright; open and slightly irregular branching. Foliage – alternate, oval to oblong, pointed, ⅓-¾ inch long. Flower – inconspicuous. Fruit – fall; berries ¼ inch diameter.
Texture	Fine.
Color	Foliage – rich, dark green. Fruit – black.
Culture	Sun or shade. Soil – medium drainage; high fertility. Moisture – medium. Pruning – withstands shearing in late winter and again in June for formal hedges. Pest Problems – spider mites. Growth Rate – slow.
Landscape Notes	Excellent for hedges, specimen, or planter boxes. Picturesque in natural form. Good substitute for boxwood. Needs part shade in Coastal Plain.

Ilex (eye'lecks)
hollies

crenata (kree-nay'ta)
scalloped or with
irregularly waved margin

'Rotundifolia' (ro-tun-di-fo'li-a)
round-leaved

ROUNDLEAF
JAPANESE HOLLY

Family Aquifoliaceae

Zones	6, 7, 8.
Size	Height 4-6 feet; spread 4-6 feet.
Form	Rounded and irregular in outline. Foliage – alternate, 1 inch long with crenate margins. Flower – inconspicuous, sterile. Fruit – none.
Texture	Medium to fine.
Color	Foliage – dark green.
Culture	Sun or shade. Soil – medium drainage; medium fertility with high organic content. Moisture – medium. Pruning – maintain size. Pest Problems – scale, spider mites, and nematodes. Growth Rate – moderate.
Landscape Notes	Suitable for foundation plantings or grouped in masses as background. May be trimmed to form hedge or accent plant. Withstands city conditions well, requiring minimum care when established.

Jasminum (jas'min-um)
   Arabic name for
   jasmine

floridum (flo'ri-dum)
   freely flowering

FLOWERING JASMINE

Family Oleaceae

Zones	7,8.
Size	Height 4-6 feet; spread 5-7 feet.
Form	Arching and rambling mound. Foliage – alternate, 3 leaflets ½-1½ inches long. Flower – May through June; ½ inch wide in clusters.
Texture	Fine.
Color	Foliage – medium green. Flower – yellow.
Culture	Sun or part shade. Soil – tolerant; medium drainage; medium fertility. Moisture – low to medium. Pruning – none. Pest Problems – none. Growth Rate – moderate.
Landscape Notes	May be trained as vine. Acts as large scale ground cover when used in mass plantings. Excellent on banks or over wall where graceful form shows to advantage. Useful for unclipped hedges or borders requiring little care once established. Interesting espaliered.

Juniperus (jew-nip'er-us)
  juniperlike

chinensis (chi-nen'sis)
  from China

pfitzeriana (fits-er-ee-ane'a)
  named for E.H.H. Pfitzer
  of Germany

PFITZER JUNIPER

Family Cupressaceae

Zones	6,7,8.
Size	Height 4-6 feet; spread 6-9 feet.
Form	Loose and graceful, medium density. Foliage – scalelike. Fruit – berries about ⅜ inch in diameter; sexes separate.
Texture	Medium to fine.
Color	Foliage – grayish green to steel-blue. Fruit – blue-gray.
Culture	Sun. Soil – tolerant; good drainage, medium fertility. Moisture – medium to low. Pruning – clip side branches for balance; allow adequate growing space. Pest Problems – bagworms, juniper scale, and spider mites. Growth Rate – fairly rapid.
Landscape Notes	Takes on rugged character with age. Best used in broad masses in large-scale areas. Exotic in appearance, does not mix well with other plants but blends nicely with rock or unpainted wood. Too large for residential foundation plantings. Grows well in Coastal Plain but is susceptible to salt burn.
Varieties	'Glauca' – silvery blue foliage. 'Nana' – dwarf form. 'Nick's Compact' – excellent compact form.

Kalmia (kal'mi-a)
   named for Peter
   Kalm, botanist

latifolia (la-ti-fo'li-a)
   broad-leaved

MOUNTAIN-LAUREL

Family Ericaceae

Zones	6, 7.
Size	Height 4-6 feet; spread 3-5 feet.
Form	Large and robust if not crowded, symmetrical and dense; in old age becomes open and loose with very picturesque trunks and limbs. Foliage – alternate, 3-5 inches long, glossy and leathery. Flower – May to June; large terminal corymbs. Fruit – fall and winter; 5-valved capsules.
Texture	Medium.
Color	Foliage – bright green. Flower – white to deep rose.
Culture	Shade or sun if moist; grows well in part shade on rocky sites near water. Soil – good drainage; medium fertility with acid humus added. Moisture – high. Pruning – none. Pest Problems – leaf miner, leaf spot, blight, aphids, borers, and lacebug. Growth Rate – slow.
Landscape Notes	Beautiful native shrub; mass on north of buildings or in dark nooks under trees. Used in foundation planting, informal borders, and on slopes. May be grown in Coastal Plain in moist cool sites.
Varieties	'Alba' – white flowers. 'Myrtifolia' – dwarf form.

Mahonia (ma-ho'ni-a)
   named for M'Mahon,
   American horticulturist

bealei (be-lea'i)
   named for T.C. Beale

LEATHERLEAF MAHONIA

Family Berberidaceae

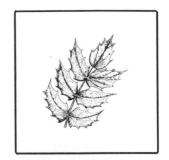

Zones	6, 7, 8.
Size	Height 5-6 feet; spread 3-4 feet.
Form	Upright and open. Foliage – alternate, 5-9 leaflets of medium density, clustered at tops of stems. Flower – late March; small, in clusters 6 inches long. Fruit – early summer; grapelike clusters.
Texture	Coarse.
Color	Foliage – bronze-green; fall, reddish-green. Flower – bright yellow. Fruit – blue.
Culture	Part shade or shade. Soil – medium drainage; medium fertility with high organic content. Moisture – medium. Pruning – heavy pruning of side branches on old or neglected plants. Pest Problems – leaf spot. Growth Rate – fairly slow.
Landscape Notes	Very dependable for use in shrub borders or as specimen. Winterburn if grown in sun. Interesting and exotic effect with contemporary structures.

Mahonia (ma-ho'ni-a)
  named for M'Mahon, American
  horticulturist

pinnata (pin-na'ta)
  pinnate

CLUSTER MAHONIA

Family Berberidaceae

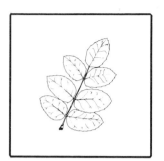

Zones	6, 7, 8.
Size	Height 4-6 feet; spread 3 feet.
Form	Thick and compact with vertical branching. Foliage – alternate, pinnately compound with 7-13 spiny leaflets. Flower – early April; terminal clusters. Fruit – summer; berry.
Texture	Medium to coarse.
Color	Foliage – dull green; winter, reddish-purple. Flower – yellow. Fruit – blue-black.
Culture	Sun to part shade. Resists cold, heat, and droughts. Soil – tolerant. Moisture – medium. Pruning – remove outer canes to promote foliage at base. Pest Problems – none. Growth Rate – slow to moderate.
Landscape Notes	Useful for border or specimen; not as limited in use as coarser textured species. Excellent vertical accent. Foliage and flowers interesting. One of few mahonias that will grow well in sun.

Myrica (mir-i'ka)
  ancient Greek, possibly
  name for Tamarisk

pensylvanica (pen-sel-va'nye-ca)
  of Pennsylvania

NORTHERN BAYBERRY

Family Myricaceae

Zones	6, 7, 8.
Size	Height 3-6 feet; spread 3-8 feet.
Form	Dense, mounded, and spreading. Foliage – alternate, leathery, oblong, 2-4 inches long, aromatic. Flower – spring; inconspicuous; sexes on separate plants. Fruit – late September, persisting through winter; ⅛ inch waxy berries on female plants.
Texture	Medium.
Color	Foliage – dark gray-green. Fruit – gray.
Culture	Sun or part shade. Soil – very tolerant. Moisture – medium to low. Pruning – tolerant. Pest Problems – none. Growth Rate – moderate.
Landscape Notes	Excellent for beach landscaping, particularly as salt wind barrier; plant 2-3 feet apart in row. May be naturalized in masses; effective in shrub borders and foundation plantings. Semi-evergreen in mountain areas. Fruit attracts birds.

Nandina (nan-dy'na)
  Japanese name

domestica (do-mes'ti-ka)
  domesticated, not wild

NANDINA

Family Berberidaceae

Zones	7,8.
Size	Height 4-6 feet; spread 2-3 feet.
Form	Upright with many canes; becomes leggy at base unless special pruning practiced; non-branching stems. Foliage – alternate, twice or three times compound, with leaflets 1-1½ inches long. Flower – April; small and single, appearing in clusters on terminal growth. Fruit – fall and winter; terminal clusters about 12 inches long.
Texture	Medium to fine.
Color	Foliage – green; winter, greenish-maroon or red. Flower – creamy white. Fruit – red.
Culture	Sun or part shade. Soil – good drainage; medium fertility with high organic content. Moisture – medium. Pruning – light pinching of tips for compactness. Heading back of canes to varying lengths for rejuvenation of old plants. Renovation accomplished in 2 to 3 years on neglected plants. Pest Problems – none. Growth Rate – moderate.
Landscape Notes	Interesting used as facer shrub or planted in groups. Avoid placing near red brick buildings. Excellent vertical accent. Good for year-round interest.
Varieties	'Alba' – white berries. 'Nana' – reaches height of 18 inches, very few berries. Good for edging.

Pieris (py-ee'ris)
    named for Greek muse

floribunda (flor-i-bun'da)
    free-flowering

MOUNTAIN ANDROMEDA

Family Ericaceae

Zones	6, 7.
Size	Height 4-6 feet; spread 3-4 feet.
Form	Stems erect, with full rounded or oval habit. Foliage – alternate, toothed, 1-3 inches long. Flower – March and April; urn-shaped, ¼ inch long in upright terminal panicles 5 inches long. Fruit – fall; dry capsules ⅓ inch long.
Texture	Medium.
Color	Foliage – dark green; new growth, reddish-green. Flower – white. Fruit – greenish-brown.
Culture	Part shade to full shade. Soil – good drainage; medium fertility with acid humus added. Moisture – medium to high. Pruning – infrequently remove older stems to encourage new growth. Pest Problems – none. Growth Rate – slow.
Landscape Notes	Hardiest of *Pieris* species to cold temperature. Flower buds formed in fall lend interest throughout winter months. Excellent as specimen or accent. Useful in foundation plantings for contemporary or traditional houses and with other evergreens in natural settings, mixed shrub borders, and groupings.
Variety	'Grandiflora' – very large flower clusters.

Pieris (py-ee'ris)
  named for
  Greek muse

japonica (ja-pon'i-ka)
  from Japan

JAPANESE ANDROMEDA

Family Ericaceae

Zones	6, 7.
Size	Height 4-6 feet; spread 4-6 feet.
Form	Upright and neat habit with stiff, spreading branches and dense rosettelike masses of foliage to ground. Foliage – alternate, in heavy whorls at ends of branches, leathery, 3 inches long. Flower – early April; terminal pendulous clusters 5 inches long, arranged to give effect of large panicles. Fruit – fall; 5 valved capsule.
Texture	Medium.
Color	Foliage – lustrous deep green; new growth rich bronze. Flower – white. Fruit – brownish.
Culture	Part shade or shade. Soil – medium drainage; high fertility with acid humus added. Moisture – high. Pruning – dead twigs. Pest Problems – lacebug and root rot in poorly drained soils. Growth Rate – slow.
Landscape Notes	Very beautiful and graceful early-blooming shrub. Useful among other broad-leaved evergreens, in shrub borders, or as specimen or mass. Needs morning sun for best flowering. Slow to reestablish when transplanted. Useful in city gardens. May be grown in Coastal Plain in moist cool sites.
Varieties	'Compacta' – small leaves, compact habit. 'Dorothy Wycoff' – dark-pink to red flowers; compact habit.

Prunus (proo'nus)
  classical Latin name
  of plum

laurocerasus (law-ro-se'ra-sus)
  classical name of laurel

angustifolia (an-gus-ti-fo'li-a)
  narrow-leaved

NARROW-LEAVED
ENGLISH LAUREL

Family Rosaceae

Zones	6, 7, 8.
Size	Height 4-6 feet; spread 5-6 feet.
Form	Low spreading with horizontal branches. Foliage – shiny and leathery; 3-4 inches long and 1 inch wide. Flower – spring; clusters. Fruit – summer; berrylike.
Texture	Medium.
Color	Foliage – medium green. Flower – white. Fruit – black.
Culture	Sun or shade. Soil – tolerates acid or alkaline; good drainage; medium fertility with high organic content. Moisture – medium. Pruning – none. Pest Problems – wood borers and leaf spot. Growth Rate – moderate.
Landscape Notes	Excellent for contemporary design. Good low growing foundation plant. Adapts well to city conditions. Often sheds foliage when transplanted.

Pyracantha (py-ra-kan'tha)
　　from Greek for fire
　　and thorn

coccinea (kok-sin'i-a)
　　scarlet

SCARLET FIRETHORN

Family Rosaceae

Zones	6, 7, 8.
Size	Height 5-6 feet; spread 6-8 feet.
Form	Upright and spreading; many trunks with thorns on branches. Foliage – alternate, 1½ inches long. Flower – early May; ⅓ inch wide in clusters. Fruit – fall and winter; ¼ inch berries in clusters distributed along branches.
Texture	Medium.
Color	Foliage – bronze green. Flower – white. Fruit – red orange.
Culture	Sun. Soil – medium to good drainage; medium fertility with high organic content. Moisture – medium. Pruning – shape; may be sheared for hedging. Pest Problems – scale, aphids, lacebug, and fire blight. Growth Rate – moderate to rapid.
Landscape Notes	Needs 3 to 4 applications general purpose spray annually starting late March or early April. Large and showy varieties now available. Use as wall shrub, specimen, or foundation planting.
Varieties	'Kasan' – outstanding for large orange-yellow berries which color in August and hold for 2 months. Leaves 1 inch long, elliptical, and shiny. Spreading habit of growth. Branches to ground. Extremely cold hardy. 'Lalandei' – hardy and widely grown. Orange fruit. Good for espalier.

Raphiolepis (raf-i-oll'ep-is)
    Greek needle scale, referring
    to bracts in inflorescence

umbellata (um-bel-lay'ta)
    with umbels

YEDDO-HAWTHORN

Family Rosaceae

Zones	7,8.
Size	Height 4-6 feet; spread 6 feet.
Form	Upright and open with stout branches. Foliage – alternate, oval to almost round, leathery, 3 inches long. Flower – May; upright panicles, fragrant. Fruit – fall and winter; berries ⅜ inch diameter.
Texture	Medium to coarse.
Color	Foliage – dark green. Flower – white. Fruit – blue-black.
Culture	Sun or part shade. Soil – tolerant; medium drainage; medium fertility. Moisture – medium. Pruning – none. Pest Problems – nematodes, scale, and blight. Growth Rate – slow.
Landscape Notes	Inclined to legginess, may need facer shrubs to look best. Fairly drought resistant. Withstands salt spray and wind.

Rhododendron (ro-do-den'dron)
   Greek for rose and tree

carolinianum (ka-ro-lin-i-a'num)
   from Carolinas

CAROLINA RHODODENDRON

Family Ericaceae

Zones	6, 7.
Size	Height 4-5 feet; spread 3-4 feet.
Form	Compact and global. Foliage – alternate, elliptic, leathery, 2-3 inches long. Flower – late April; about 1½ inches wide, fragrant.
Texture	Medium.
Color	Foliage – blue-green, brownish beneath. Flower – pink to white.
Culture	Sun or part shade. Soil – very good drainage; medium fertility with high acid organic content. Moisture – medium to high. Pruning – promote denseness. Pest Problems – root rot. Growth Rate – moderate.
Landscape Notes	Good for Western Carolina. Fine as individual specimen or in masses. Rugged and picturesque form with interesting twig structure. Pleasing but unspectacular flowering. Useful in foundation plantings.
Variety	'Album' – white flowers; popular and reliable.

Rhododendron (ro-do-den'dron)
Greek for rose and tree

hybrida (hy'brid-a)
hybrid

HYBRID RHODODENDRON

Family Ericaceae

Zones	6, 7, 8.
Size	Height 4-6 feet; spread 3-5 feet.
Form	Rounded or spreading depending on variety and exposure. Foliage – alternate, 3-5 inches, leathery, narrow-oblong to obovate, usually acute at tip. Flower – May; borne in trusses. Fruit – fall; capsules.
Texture	Medium to coarse.
Color	Foliage – medium to dark green. Flower – white, pink, red, purple.
Culture	Sun to part shade. Soil – very good drainage; medium fertility. Moisture – medium to high. Pruning – increase denseness. Pest Problems – root rot, lacebug, and spider mites. Growth Rate – slow to moderate.
Landscape Notes	Distinguished as specimen or in borders and foundation plantings; grows well under pines or oaks or with exposure to sun and wind. When established needs little care.
Varieties	'America' – dark red flowers. 'Anna Rose Whitney' – pink flowers. Vigorous tall grower with large leaves. 'Cheer' – flowers pink with conspicuous scarlet-red blotches. Compact low grower.

Siphonosmanthus (si-phon-os-man'thus)
    Greek for tube and
    osmanthus

delavayi (de-lay-vay'eye)
    named for Delavay,
    French missionary and botanist

DELAVAY TEA OLIVE

Family Oleaceae

Zones	7,8.
Size	Height 4-6 feet; spread 3-5 feet.
Form	Upright, twiggy, branches arching. Foliage – opposite, toothed, ½-1 inch long. Flower – April; ½ inch long in axil of leaves, fragrant. Fruit – summer; berry ½ inch long.
Texture	Fine.
Color	Foliage – glossy, deep green. Flower – white. Fruit – blue-black.
Culture	Sun or part shade. Soil – good drainage; medium fertility with humus added. Moisture – medium. Pruning – none. Pest Problems – none. Growth Rate – slow.
Landscape Notes	Excellent specimen, accent, foundation planting, natural or sheared hedge. Attractive as espalier. Foliage handsome and fragrant flowers attractive. Excellent substitute for common boxwood in lower Piedmont and Coastal Plain. Frequently listed as *Osmanthus delavayi*.

Taxus (tack'us)
   classical Latin
   name of yew

cuspidata (kus-pi-day'ta)
   having sharp, stiff
   point

JAPANESE YEW

Family Taxaceae

Zones	6, 7.
Size	Height 4-6 feet; spread 5-7 feet.
Form	Vase-shaped with open center. Foliage – needlelike, 1 inch long, loose. Flower – inconspicuous. Fruit – fall; ½ inch long, berrylike, on female plants, seed very poisonous.
Texture	Fine to medium.
Color	Foliage – light to dark green. Fruit – red.
Culture	Part shade or shade. Soil – tolerant; good drainage; medium fertility. Moisture – medium to high. Pruning – mid June; light shearing to maintain size. Pest Problems – spider mites. Growth Rate – slow.
Landscape Notes	Excellent shrub for hedges, screens, or foundation plantings; especially valuable for city gardens. Grows in variety of soils and tolerates poor growing conditions. Thrives in cool, moist sites.
Varieties	'Jeffrey's Pyramidal' – pyramidal form with heavy fruiting. 'Nana' – smaller than species, 2-3 feet in height. 'Thayerae' – wide-spreading form without open center of species.

Viburnum (vy-bur'num)
   classical Latin name
   of wayfaring tree

suspensum (sus-pen'sum)
   hung or suspended

SANDANKWA VIBURNUM

Family Caprifoliaceae

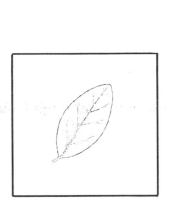

Zone	8.
Size	Height 4-6 feet; spread 4-6 feet.
Form	Erect shrub with arching branches. Foliage – opposite, rounded, leathery, 2-5 inches long. Flower – April; dense clusters 1½ inches wide, fragrant. Fruit – fall; drupe.
Texture	Coarse.
Color	Foliage – dark green. Flower – white tinged with rose. Fruit – red.
Culture	Sun or shade. Soil – tolerant; medium drainage; medium fertility with high organic content. Moisture – medium to high. Pruning – none. Pest Problems – none. Growth Rate – moderate.
Landscape Notes	Excellent specimen or accent shrub. Suitable for foundation planting and shrub borders in formal or informal settings. Not hardy in mountain area.

Yucca (yuk'ka)
   Latinized version of
   Spanish vernacular for
   some other desert plant

gloriosa (glo-ri-o'sa)
   glory or climbing lily

MOUND-LILY YUCCA

Family Liliaceae

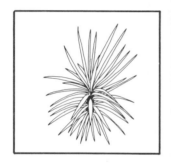

Zones	7, 8.
Size	Height 4-6 feet; spread 3-4 feet.
Form	Short trunked or no trunk. Foliage – 2-2½ feet long, 2 inches wide, stiff points, smooth margin. Flower – September; 4 inches wide in large panicles on spikes of 6-8 feet, fragrant. Fruit – November and December; capsule.
Texture	Coarse.
Color	Foliage – dark green. Flower – greenish-white to reddish. Fruit – black.
Culture	Sun. Soil – good drainage; low fertility. Moisture – low. Pruning – remove dead leaves; lower leaves may be removed to form trunk. Pest Problems – none. Growth Rate – rapid after established.
Landscape Notes	Resistant to salt spray. Frequently seen grouped with smaller growing yuccas. Sharp, stiff leaves hazardous. Combines well with santolina.

SHRUBS 4-6 FEET — DECIDUOUS

Azalea (a-zay'lee-a)
   showy shrubs,
   botonically Rhododendrons

molle (mol'le)
   softly hairy

hybrida (hy'brid-a)
   hybrid

MOLLIS AZALEA

Family Ericaceae

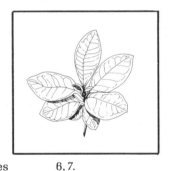

Zones	6, 7.
Size	Height 3-5 feet; spread 3-5 feet.
Form	Low spreading with well-shaped, symmetrical head resembling dwarf Rhododendron. Foliage – mid-spring to mid-fall; alternate, 2-4 inches long, white-hairy below, large and soft. Flower – early spring before leaves; large and showy, to 3½ inches, single. Fruit – late summer; dry dehiscent capsule.
Texture	Medium.
Color	Foliage – blue-green; fall, rich red or bronze. Flower – white, yellow, red, and many combinations.
Culture	Shade or part sun. Soil – good drainage; medium fertility with acid humus added; avoid manure. Moisture – high. Pruning – none. Pest Problems – spider mites, lacebug, and mildew. Growth Rate – slow.
Landscape Notes	Excellent habit and good foliage; useful in groups and mass. Not for Coastal Plain. Correct botanical name *Rhododendron kosterianum*.
Varieties	'C.B. Van Nes' – fire-red flowers. 'Consul Ceresole' – rose flowers, 3½ inch diameter.

Berberis (ber'ber-iss)
   Arabic name

thunbergii (thun-berg'ee-eye)
   named for C.P. Thunberg

JAPANESE BARBERRY

Family Berberidaceae

Zones	6, 7, 8.
Size	Height 3-5 feet; spread 3-5 feet.
Form	Globe; medium to very dense with many thorns. Foliage – alternate, simple, entire, ½-1½ inches long, without marginal teeth. Flower – mid-April; small, cup-shaped, ½ inch diameter. Fruit – fall; berry-shaped, ½ inch long. Twigs – deeply grooved with unbranched thorns.
Texture	Medium.
Color	Foliage – medium green; maroon red on red leaf varieties; fall, scarlet. Flower – creamy white. Fruit – orange-red.
Culture	Sun to part shade. Soil – tolerant; medium drainage; medium fertility. Moisture – medium. Pruning – none. Pest Problems – limited. Growth Rate – moderate.
Landscape Notes	Grows in any situation, particularly good for poor soil, shade, and exposed places. Good for use as impenetrable hedge. Tolerates exposure.
Varieties	*atropurpurea* – dark red leaves. 'Crimson Pygmy' – shrub to 1½ feet in height. Foliage red. Best color in full sun; as low hedge needs no clipping.

Chaenomeles (kee-nom'e-lees)
    Greek meaning split apple

speciosa (spee-si-o'sa)
    showy

FLOWERING QUINCE

Family Rosaceae

Zones	6, 7, 8.
Size	Height 5-6 feet; spread 5-6 feet.
Form	Semiglobe, dense. Foliage – alternate, 2-3 inches long, finely toothed. Flower – March, before leaves; 1½-2 inch diameter, single or double. Fruit – summer; applelike, 2 inches long.
Texture	Medium.
Color	Foliage – glossy green. Flower – rose-pink, scarlet, orange-red, and white. Fruit – greenish-yellow.
Culture	Sun or part shade. Soil – medium drainage; medium fertility. Moisture – medium. Pruning – annual thinning of old canes and sucker growth. Pest Problems – fire blight, scale, and aphids on new growth. Growth Rate – fairly rapid.
Landscape Notes	One of the showiest of flowering shrubs. Splendid mass with fine foliage, showy flowers, and interesting winter color; excellent for borders, specimen, or hedges. Avoid using near orchards. Interesting espaliered. Formerly known as *C. lagenaria.*
Varieties	'Cardinalis' – bright red double flowers. 'Phyllis Moore' – semi-double pink flowers. 'Snow' – single white flowers.

Hamamelis (ham-am-ee'lis)
  Greek for together and apple;
  flowers and fruit are produced at
  same time

vernalis (ver-nal'is)
  of spring

VERNAL WITCH-HAZEL

Family Hamamelidac

Zones	6, 7, 8.
Size	Height 4-6 feet; spread 2-3 feet.
Form	Dense with irregular horizontal branching. Foliage – alternate, 3-5 inches long. Flower – February to March; ½ inch wide with 4 petals, very fragrant. Fruit – dry capsule.
Texture	Coarse.
Color	Foliage – medium green; fall, bright yellow. Flower – yellow to red-brown. Fruit – brown with black seeds.
Culture	Sun or part shade. Soil – medium drainage; medium fertility with humus added. Moisture – medium to high. Pruning – none. Pest Problems – none. Growth Rate – rapid.
Landscape Notes	Useful for borders, low screens, and for naturalizing.

Hydrangea (hy-dran'jee-a)
  hardy shrubs, vines

quercifolia (quer-ki-fo'li-a)
  oaklike leaves

OAKLEAF HYDRANGEA

Family Saxifragaceae

Zones	6, 7, 8.
Size	Height 4-6 feet; spread 3-5 feet.
Form	Spreading and irregular in shape. Foliage – opposite, 3-8 inches long, 3-8 inches wide, 3-7 lobed. Flower – June; 4-12 inch erect panicles.
Texture	Coarse.
Color	Foliage – dark green above, light green beneath; fall, orange-red. Flower – white, purplish at maturity.
Culture	Part shade. Soil – medium drainage; high fertility with organic matter added. Moisture – high. Pruning – shape; remove old flower heads. Pest Problems – powdery mildew. Growth Rate – rapid.
Landscape Notes	Strong-textured accent or specimen for large scale gardens and parks. Excellent flowers and fall foliage color.

Kerria (kerr'ia)
  named for William Kerr,
  Kew gardener and collector

japonica (ja-pon'i-ka)
  from Japan

KERRIA

Family Rosaceae

Zones	6, 7, 8.
Size	Height 4-6 feet; spread 3-5 feet.
Form	Upright with slender, graceful stems. Double flowered variety some-what arching. Foliage – alternate, thin, 2 inches long, double-toothed. Flower – April; single, 1½ 2 inches wide.
Texture	Medium.
Color	Foliage – light green; fall, yellow. Flower – yellow. Twig – green.
Culture	Sun or part shade. Single flowered varieties may fade in sun. Soil – tolerant; good drainage; medium fertility. Moisture – medium. Prun-ing – remove old stems and winterkilled parts. Pest Problems – Japanese beetle, leaf and twig blight. Growth Rate – moderate.
Landscape Notes	Useful in small groups in foreground of shrub border. Attractive against walls and fences that contrast in color and texture. Can be trained as vine and used in natural areas. Little care required.
Variety	'Pleniflora' – Globe Flower. Abundant double flowers on arching branches.

Rosa (ro'za)
old Latin name
for rose

multiflora (mul-ti-flo'ra)
many or profusely
flowered

JAPANESE ROSE

Family Rosaceae

Zones	6, 7, 8.
Size	Height 4-6 feet; spread 10-15 feet.
Form	Fountain with long, slender, curving branches scattered with slender prickles. Foliage – alternate, 5-9 leaflets, soft, finely wrinkled. Flower – late spring; ¾ inch large panicles, very numerous. Fruit – summer and fall, lasting to spring; small, ovoid hips ¼ inch diameter in large clusters.
Texture	Medium to fine.
Color	Foliage – bright green. Flower – white. Fruit – red. Bark – reddish.
Culture	Sun. Soil – good drainage; medium fertility. Moisture – medium. Pruning – occasionally remove old and weak wood. Pest Problems – aphids and mildew. Growth Rate – rapid.
Landscape Notes	May be used over fences and walls and on trellises but requires much space. Forms impenetrable wide hedge.
Varieties	*cathayensis* – pale pink flowers. 'Inermis' – thornless branches.

Rosa (ro'za)
old Latin name
for rose

rugosa (roo-go'sa)
rugose, rough

RUGOSE ROSE

Family Rosaceae

Zones	6, 7, 8.
Size	Height 4-6 feet; spread 4-6 feet.
Form	Very sturdy with stout upright prickly stems covering ground and forming fairly dense mass. Foliage – alternate, 5-9 leaflets 1½-2 inches long, rough and thick with conspicuous veins. Flower – early summer through fall; 3½ inches wide, singly or in clusters, fragrant. Fruit – summer and fall; large, showy hips.
Texture	Medium.
Color	Foliage – bright green; fall, brilliant orange. Flower – purplish-rose to white. Fruit – orange-red.
Culture	Sun. Soil – good drainage; medium fertility. Moisture – medium. Pruning – remove old and dead branches and suckers. Pest Problems – borers. Growth Rate – rapid.
Landscape Notes	Handsome and useful in flower and shrub borders; numerous hybridizations. Especially suited for coastal and windy sites.
Varieties	'Albo-plena' – double white flowers. 'Rosea' – single Persian-rose flowers.

Spiraea (spy-ree'a)
Greek for wreath
or garland

cantoniensis (kan-ton-i-en'sis)
from China

REEVES SPIREA

Family Rosaceae

Zones	6, 7, 8.
Size	Height 4-6 feet; spread 3-5 feet.
Form	Upright branches flowing gracefully toward ground. Foliage – alternate, simple, 1-2½ inches long, wedge-shaped at base, deeply toothed. Flower – late May and early June; double, abundant in rounded clusters of 1-2 inch diameter.
Texture	Medium to fine.
Color	Foliage – slightly blue-green resembling *S. vanhouttei*; underside pale. Flower – pure white.
Culture	Sun or part shade. Soil – tolerant; medium drainage; medium fertility. Moisture – medium. Pruning – remove dead or injured canes. Pest Problems – aphids. Growth Rate – rapid.
Landscape Notes	Probably best spirea in Southeast. Excellent landscape plant. Easily transplanted. Use as specimen or accent plant or in shrub borders. Almost evergreen in warmer areas.

Spiraea (spy-ree'a)
Greek for wreath
or garland

thunbergii (thun-berg'ee-eye)
named for C.P. Thunberg

THUNBERG SPIREA

Family Rosaceae

Zones	6, 7, 8.
Size	Height 3-5 feet; spread 3-4 feet.
Form	Upright with thin branches recurving toward ground; fairly dense. Foliage – alternate, ¾-1½ inches long, linear and sharply toothed. Flower – February and March; single in profuse clusters 1-2 inches wide.
Texture	Very fine.
Color	Foliage – light yellow-green, pale beneath; fall, orange-red. Flower – white.
Culture	Sun or part shade. Soil – medium drainage; medium fertility. Moisture – medium. Pruning – annual thinning of old canes and weak growth to ground after flowering. Pest Problems – aphids. Growth Rate – rapid.
Landscape Notes	Earliest blooming of spireas. Graceful and delicate in appearance. Foliage retained until late November.

Vaccinium (vak-sin'i-um)
    Latin for blueberry

ashei (ash'e-eye)
    named for W. W. Ashe,
    botanist

RABBITEYE BLUEBERRY

Family Ericaceae

Zones	7, 8.
Size	Height 4-6 feet; spread 3-5 feet.
Form	Globe to semiglobe with upright canes. Foliage – alternate, simple, 2-4 inches long. Flower – early spring; small but showy. Fruit – July to August; edible berries about ½ inch diameter.
Texture	Medium.
Color	Foliage – glossy green to powdery green; fall, dull green to bright red. Flower – white. Fruit – sky blue.
Culture	Sun. Soil – good drainage; medium fertility with low pH (5 or lower) and high organic matter; mulch with 4 inches sawdust, peat, or pine bark. Moisture – medium. Pruning – yearly or according to variety requirements. Pest Problems – spider mites, leafhoppers, and thrips. Growth Rate – moderate.
Landscape Notes	Excellent as informal hedge or border. Protect fruit from birds by enclosing plants. Highbush types *(V. corymbosum)* are not generally recommended for home plantings because of exacting soil requirements.
Varieties	'Tifblue' – midseason, large fruit; large plant. 'Woodard' – early fruit; small plant.

SHRUBS 6-12 FEET — EVERGREEN

Azalea (a-zay'lee-a)
   showy shrubs, botanically
   Rhododendrons

indica (in'di-ka)
   from India

INDIAN AZALEA

Family Ericaceae

Zones	7, 8.
Size	Height 6-12 feet; spread 6-8 feet.
Form	Spreading or upright depending on variety. Foliage – alternate, simple, pubescent, 1-2 inches long. Flower – late March to mid-April; 2-3 inch diameter. Stems – hairy.
Texture	Medium.
Color	Foliage – dark green. Flower – depends on variety.
Culture	Sun or shade. Soil – good drainage; medium fertility with high acid organic content. Moisture – high. Pruning – occasional thinning. Pest Problems – lacebug, spider mites, petal blight, and root rot. Growth Rate – moderate.
Landscape Notes	Best in Coastal Plain and warmer parts of Piedmont. Requires mulch. Easy to transplant.
Varieties	'Fielders White' – flowers white with faint chartreuse blotch, single, frilled, 2¾ inch diameter. Spreading growth. 'Formosa' – flowers purple, single, 3 inch diameter. Upright growth. Not cold hardy in Piedmont.

Bambusa (bam-boo'sa)
  Latinized version
  of Malayan vernacular

multiplex (mul'ti-plex)
  many-folded

HEDGE BAMBOO

Family Poaceae

Zones	7,8.
Size	Height 10-12 feet; spread 4-6 feet.
Form	Slightly arching with many branches developing successively in year from crowded basal nodes of earlier branches. Foliage – alternate; 6 inches long, flat, glabrous.
Texture	Medium.
Color	Foliage – green; silver on underside.
Culture	Sun or shade. Soil – tolerant; medium drainage; medium fertility with organic matter added. Moisture – high. Pruning – none. Pest Problems – none. Growth Rate – rapid.
Landscape Notes	Clump bamboo which remains confined to limited area, unlike many bamboos which spread rapidly and require confinement of root system. Use in hedges, screens, and as tubbed specimen. Plant divisions only in spring, or from containers any time. Not hardy in mountain areas. Often listed as *B. disticha*.

Buxus (buck'us)
  classical Latin
  for box

sempervirens (sem-per-vy'renz)
  evergreen

arborescens (ar-bore-ress'ens)
  becoming treelike

TREE BOXWOOD

Family Buxaceae

Zones	6, 7.
Size	Height 8-12 feet; spread 8-10 feet.
Form	Round and formal. Foliage – opposite, 1¼ inch, narrow and spaced well apart on twigs with leaf points forming rounded triangle. Flower – inconspicuous. Fruit – inconspicuous.
Texture	Fine.
Color	Foliage – dark green.
Culture	Part shade. Soil – fairly tolerant; medium drainage; medium fertility. Moisture – medium. Pruning – light shearing annually to promote compact growth; remove dead twigs and debris from center annually to prevent fungus growth. Pest Problems – leaf miner, nematodes, and scale insects. Growth Rate – medium.
Landscape Notes	Vigorous and hardy shrub for cooler sections. Best used as tall screen for parks or large properties. Requires little care when established except for mulching and shelter from wind and winter sun.

Callistemon (kal-iss-tee'mon)
Greek for *kalos*, beauty, and
stemon, stamen

lanceolatus (lan-se-o-lay'tus)
shaped like lance head

BOTTLEBRUSH

Family Myrtaceae

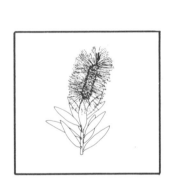

Zone	8.
Size	Height 6-12 feet; spread to 8 feet.
Form	Dense with upright branching. Foliage – alternate, simple, entire, 3 inches long, leathery, lanceolate. Flower – April to May; 2-4 inch spikes with numerous stamens 1 inch long. Fruit – woody capsule.
Texture	Fine.
Color	Foliage – medium to light green. Flower – bright red. Fruit – light brown.
Culture	Sun. Soil – tolerant; withstands drought. Moisture – low. Pruning – none. Pest Problems – none. Growth Rate – moderate.
Landscape Notes	Grown primarily for floral display. Best placed in front of evergreen background. Fruit useful in dried arrangements. In very warm areas may be trained as specimen tree. Good screening material for protected beach properties.

Camellia (ka-me'li-a)
    named for
    George J. Kamel

japonica (ja-pon'i-ka)
    from Japan

CAMELLIA

Family Theaceae

Zones	7,8.
Size	Height 7-12 feet; spread 5-7 feet.
Form	Usually upright with slightly pyramidal form. Foliage – alternate, to 4 inches long. Flower – late August to May, depending on variety; 2-6 inches across.
Texture	Medium.
Color	Foliage – glossy dark green. Flower – white, pink, red, or varigated.
Culture	Part shade; plant on northern exposure if in full sun. Soil – good drainage; medium fertility with humus added. Moisture – medium. Pruning – shape. Remove faded flowers. Pest Problems – scale, dieback, and root rot. Growth Rate – rapid.
Landscape Notes	Easily grown but very formal in character, suitable as specimen in large gardens. Hundreds of varieties available. Requires protection from winter wind. Mulch. May be used as background or espalier. Subject to chlorosis from iron deficiency.
Varieties	'Frau Minna Seidel' – pink double flowers; suitable for small gardens. 'Imura' – semidouble white flowers; reliable.

Camellia (ka-mee'li-a)
　　named for
　　George J. Kamel

sasanqua (sass-ann'qua)
　　from Japanese
　　vernacular name

SASANQUA CAMELLIA

Family Theaceae

Zones	7, 8.
Size	Height 7-12 feet; spread 5-7 feet.
Form	Upright, columnar, compact or open and spreading. Foliage – alternate, to 2 inches long. Flower – October through January depending on variety; single or double, 2-3½ inches wide.
Texture	Medium.
Color	Foliage – lustrous dark green. Flower – depends on variety.
Culture	Sun to part shade. Soil – good drainage; low to medium fertility, slightly acid. Moisture – medium. Pruning – none. Pest Problems – scale and root rot. Growth Rate – rapid.
Landscape Notes	Excellent for informal borders, specimen, accent, and sheared or natural hedges. If not planted in shade, should be planted where morning sun does not strike foliage. Overgrown specimens may be trimmed to multitrunk small tree.
Varieties	'Appleblossom' – flowers white edged pink, single. Upright rapid growth; excellent for tall hedges and screens. 'Cleopatra' – flowers rose-pink, semidouble. Rapid compact growth, excellent for hedges.

Cleyera (clay'er-a)
  named for
  Andrew Cleyer

japonica (ja-pon'i-ka)
  from Japan

CLEYERA

Family Theaceae

Zones	7,8.
Size	Height 8-10 feet; spread 5-6 feet.
Form	Upright and billowing. Foliage – alternate, 2-6 inches long, oblong, veinless, and minutely serrate at apex. Flower – spring; fragrant, about ½ inch across. Fruit – fall; globose to ovoid berry.
Texture	Medium.
Color	Foliage – glossy reddish-bronze to green. Flower – white. Fruit – red.
Culture	Part shade. Soil – very good drainage; medium to low fertility with organic matter added. Moisture – medium to high. Pruning – shape. Pest Problems – none. Growth Rate – moderate.
Landscape Notes	Hardy through Piedmont and Coastal Plain. Highly shade tolerant; withstands city conditions. Excellent for large shrub borders and screens or as specimen or patio planting when trimmed to multi-trunk tree form. Ideal for narrow places and formal or informal hedge. Excellent along coast but must be protected from salt spray. Often listed as *Eurya ochnacea*.

Elaeagnus (eel-ee-ag'nus)
  from Greek for olive
  and chaste tree

pungens (pun'jenz)
  piercing, sharp pointed

THORNY ELAEAGNUS
Family Elaeagnaceae

Zones	7,8.
Size	Height 8-11 feet; spread 6-10 feet.
Form	Spreading and dense with pendulous branches. Readily trimmed to compact, ovate or globose form. Foliage – alternate, 1½-3 inches long, oblong-ovate. Flower – October; ½ inch long, inconspicuous, very fragrant. Fruit – April; elliptical, inconspicuous.
Texture	Medium.
Color	Foliage – glossy, bright green, silvery beneath. Flower – silvery-white. Fruit – rusty-brown.
Culture	Sun. Soil – very tolerant; medium drainage; low to medium fertility. Moisture – low. Pruning – tolerant. Pest Problems – spider mites during summer. Growth Rate – rapid.
Landscape Notes	Effective as large scale specimen, natural hedge, shrub border, covering on banks. One of few plants having winter flowering and spring fruiting. Gardenia scented flowers. Tolerant of many adverse conditions such as salt spray. Espaliers well against dark background. Fruit attracts birds.
Variety	'Fruitland' – symmetrical in habit; leaves slightly larger than species, silvery beneath.

Euonymus (you-on'i-mus)
   hardy shrubs and vines

japonicus (ja-pon'i-kus)
   from Japan

EVERGREEN EUONYMUS

Family Celastraceae

Zones	7, 8.
Size	Height 6-7 feet; spread 3-5 feet.
Form	Compact in sun, spreading in shade. Foliage – opposite, thick, slightly serrated, 1-3 inches long, waxy. Flower – early summer; clusters, inconspicuous. Fruit – late summer and fall, often failing to develop; capsule with 4 seeds.
Texture	Medium.
Color	Foliage – dark green. Flower – white. Fruit – pink to red. Stem – green.
Culture	Sun or shade. Soil – medium drainage; medium fertility with high organic content. Moisture – medium. Pruning – none. Pest Problems – anthracnose, crown gall, leaf spots, aphids, and scale. Growth Rate – rapid.
Landscape Notes	Formerly used widely as specimen shrub and in hedges. Prevention and control of insects and disease limits desirability. Tolerates salt spray.
Variety	'Albo-marginatus' – white margins on leaves.

Feijoa (fy-jo'a)
   subtropical fruit;
   pineapple guava

sellowiana (sel-lo-wi-a'na)
   named for Friedrich Sello,
   German traveler in South
   America

PINEAPPLE GUAVA

Family Myrtaceae

Zone	8.
Size	Height 10-18 feet; spread to 10 feet.
Form	Loose and open with spreading or slightly horizontal branching. Foliage – opposite, entire, 2-3 inches long, oval-oblong. Flower – May; 1¼ inch diameter. Fruit fall; 1-3 inches long, egg-shaped, edible.
Texture	Medium.
Color	Foliage – gray-green with silver beneath. Flower – white to reddish. Fruit – green, tinged red, turning pale yellow.
Culture	Sun. Soil – good drainage; medium fertility with humus added. Moisture – low. Pruning – maintain shape. Pest Problems – none. Growth Rate – rapid.
Landscape Notes	Valuable for loose, open appearance in screens and borders or clipped as hedge. Subject to cold damage in mountain areas and Piedmont, hardy to 10°.
Variety	'Variegata' — leaves green with cream.

Ilex (eye'lecks)
    hollies

aquifolium (a-kwi-fo'li-um)
    holly-leaved

ENGLISH HOLLY

Family Aquifoliaceae

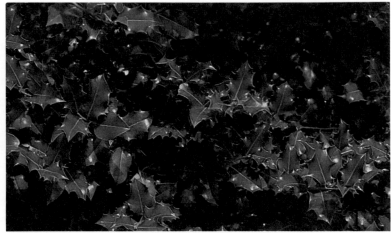

Zones	6, 7.
Size	Height 8-12 feet; spread 7-12 feet.
Form	Conical in youth, becoming more irregular and loose with age, more dense than *I. opaca*. Branches to ground. Foliage – alternate, 1½-3 inches long, wavy-margined with large triangular teeth, inclined to curl and very spiny. Flower – spring; on previous year's wood; fragrant, inconspicuous. Fruit – fall; ¼ inch globose drupes in large clusters.
Texture	Medium.
Color	Foliage – shiny dark green. Flower – dull-whitish. Fruit – bright red. Bark – pale gray.
Culture	Sun or part shade. Soil – medium drainage; medium fertility. Moisture – medium. Pruning – tolerant when mature. Pest Problems – cottony cushion scale. Growth Rate – slow.
Landscape Notes	Both male and female plants necessary for fruiting. Handsome foliage; useful as specimen, mass, or hedge in areas having moist atmosphere. Susceptible to cold injury in mountains. Foliage with long-lasting fruit excellent for Christmas decorations.
Varieties	*angustifolia* – small narrow leaves. 'Camelliaefolia' – fewer spines on leaves; large red fruit.

Ilex (eye'lecks)
  hollies

cornuta (kor-new'ta)
  horned

CHINESE HOLLY

Family Aquifoliaceae

Zones	7, 8.
Size	Height 8-10 feet; spread 5-7 feet.
Form	Rounded and upright with medium density. Foliage – alternate, 1½-5 inches long with 4-5 spines. Flower – inconspicuous. Fruit – late summer and fall; ⅜ inch diameter in large clusters.
Texture	Medium to slightly coarse.
Color	Foliage – medium green. Fruit – red or yellow.
Culture	Sun or part shade. Soil – medium to good drainage; medium fertility with high organic content. Moisture – medium. Pruning – sometimes needed for control of form. Pest Problems – scale. Growth Rate – moderate.
Landscape Notes	Partly self-fruitful; transplants with some degree of difficulty. Useful as hedge or massive foundation plant. Ragged appearance when sheared.

Ilex (eye'lecks)
  hollies

cornuta (kor-new'ta)
  horned

'Burfordii' (burr'ferd-eye)
  from Mr. Burford, Atlanta, Georgia

BURFORD HOLLY

Family Aquifoliaceae

Zones	6, 7, 8.
Size	Height 8-15 feet; spread 6-8 feet.
Form	Large, globose, dense and bushy; branches drooping. Foliage – alternate, 1½-4 inches, cupped with no or few spines, usually one on tip. Flower – inconspicuous. Fruit – fall and winter; heavily fruiting, ⅜ inch diameter berry.
Texture	Medium.
Color	Foliage – dark green with waxy sheen. Fruit – orange-red.
Culture	Sun or part shade. Soil – tolerant. Moisture – medium. Pruning – none. Pest Problems – usually none; black mildew, leaf spot, scale, and holly leaf miner occasionally. Growth Rate – rapid.
Landscape Notes	Widely used in landscaping. Excellent plant for formal or informal hedge or specimen for spacious areas and large buildings. Attractive as multistem small tree. Tolerates salt spray.
Variety	'Nana'– dwarf form with same characteristics. Height 4-5 feet; spread 3-4 feet. Excellent for foundation or hedge plantings.

Ilex (eye'lecks)
  hollies

crenata (kree-nay'ta)
  scalloped or with
  irregularly waved
  margin

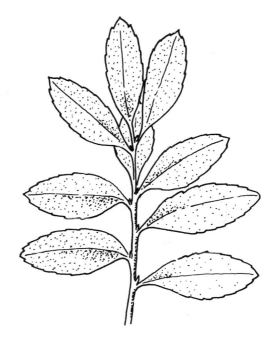

JAPANESE HOLLY

Family Aquifoliaceae

Zones	6, 7, 8.
Size	Height 10-12 feet; spread 3-5 feet.
Form	Semiglobular. Foliage – alternate, simple, toothed, ⅝ to 1¼ inches long. Flower – inconspicuous. Fruit – late summer and fall; stalked berries ¼ inch diameter.
Texture	Medium.
Color	Foliage – dark green. Fruit – black.
Culture	Sun or part shade. Soil – medium drainage; medium fertility with high organic content. Moisture – medium. Pruning – none. Pest Problems – scale, spider mites, and nematodes. Growth Rate – fairly slow.
Landscape Notes	Male and female plants necessary to produce berries. Suitable for screening or hedging. Dozens of variations in form and foliage from this species. Useful as background material.
Variety	*latifolia* – glossy leaves 1½ inches long and ½ inch wide. Vigorous upright growth to 12-16 feet.

Ilex (eye'lecks)
  hollies

glabra (glay'bra)
  smooth

INKBERRY HOLLY

Family Aquifoliaceae

Zones	6, 7, 8.
Size	Height 6-9 feet; spread 4-7 feet.
Form	Upright, semiglobular. Foliage – alternate, simple, entire or with few obtuse teeth toward apex, glabrous, 1-2 inches long. Flower – May; inconspicuous. Fruit – late summer and fall; ¼ inch single berries on female plants.
Texture	Medium.
Color	Foliage – lustrous dark green. Fruit – black.
Culture	Sun or shade. Soil – medium drainage; medium fertility with high organic content. Moisture – medium. Pruning – none. Pest Problems – scale. Growth Rate – slow to moderate.
Landscape Notes	Select male plants for best winter color. Native to coastal regions of Southeast. Most useful as background plant. Excellent material for naturalizing.
Variety	'Compacta' – dwarf female clone; height 3-3½ feet; spread 3½-4 feet. Excellent foundation or informal hedge plant. May be used as filler with flowering shrubs.

Ilex (eye'lecks)
hollies

latifolia (la-ti-fo'li-a)
broad-leaved

LUSTERLEAF HOLLY

Family Aquifoliaceae

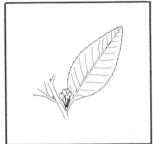

Zones	7, 8.
Size	Height 8-12 feet; spread 7-11 feet.
Form	Dense and rounded. Foliage – alternate, 4-8 inches long, thick and leathery with serrated margins. Flower – inconspicuous; sexes separate. Fruit – fall and winter; berries ⅓ inch diameter in crowded clusters.
Texture	Coarse.
Color	Foliage – lustrous dark green. Fruit – dull red.
Culture	Part shade. Soil – good drainage; medium fertility with high organic content. Moisture – medium to high. Pruning – maintain desired size. Pest Problems – none. Growth Rate – moderate.
Landscape Notes	Handsome evergreen. Use in large scale shrub borders; excellent for industrial or park sites or as specimen or screening plant for large areas. Small tree at maturity.

Ilex (eye'lecks)
   hollies

pernyi (pern'ee-i)
   named for Paul Perny

PERNY HOLLY

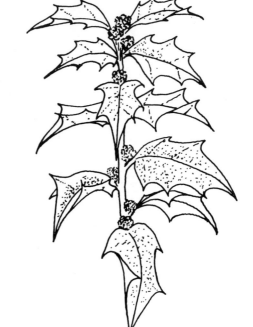

Family Aquifoliaceae

Zones	6, 7, 8.
Size	Height 9-12 feet; spread 4-6 feet.
Form	Pyramidal outline with twigs drooping and graceful, rare for hollies. Foliage – alternate, ½-1 inch long with irregular spines. Fruit – fall and winter; clusters of berries ¼ inch diameter.
Texture	Medium.
Color	Foliage – light green. Fruit – red.
Culture	Sun or part shade. Soil – tolerant; medium drainage; medium fertility. Moisture – medium. Pruning – none. Pest Problems – none. Growth Rate – slow.
Landscape Notes	Taller growing than many shrub hollies. Valued for showy red fruit.
Variety	*veitchii* – leaves 2 inches long.

Ilex (eye'lecks)
  hollies

vomitoria (vom-i-tor'i-a)
  emetic

YAUPON HOLLY

Family Aquifoliaceae

Zones	7,8.
Size	Height 5-15 feet; spread 6-12 feet.
Form	Upright, irregular large shrub to small tree. Foliage – alternate, to 1 inch long, leathery, similar to *I. crenata*. Flower – inconspicuous, separate sexes. Fruit – fall and winter; small single berries.
Texture	Medium to fine.
Color	Foliage – gray-green. Fruit – translucent red. Bark – whitish-gray.
Culture	Sun or shade. Soil – tolerant; medium drainage; medium fertility. Moisture – medium. Pruning – may be shaped for special growth habits; picturesque with multiple trunk; tolerates shearing. Pest Problems – none. Growth Rate – slow to moderate.
Landscape Notes	Highly versatile shrub or small tree which adapts to most adverse conditions. Useful as border, screen, specimen, or barrier for large properties. May be clipped to form low or high hedge or multitrunk small tree. Susceptible to salt burn. Fruit attracts birds.
Variety	'Pendula' – weeping habit. For specimen or accent.

Illicium (il-li'si-um)
Latin for something
enticing, in allusion
to pleasant aroma

anisatum (a-ni-say'tum)
anise-scented

ANISETREE

Family Magnoliaceae

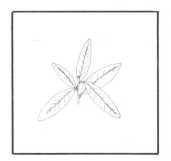

Zones	7,8.
Size	Height 8-12 feet; spread 8-10 feet.
Form	Open and rounded. Foliage – alternate, 2-3 inches long, leathery and aromatic. Flower – July; 1 inch diameter, not fragrant. Fruit – fall; follicles arranged in star shape.
Texture	Medium to coarse.
Color	Foliage – olive green. Flower – greenish-yellow. Fruit – brown.
Culture	Sun or part shade. Soil – medium drainage; high fertility. Moisture – medium to high. Pruning – none. Pest Problems – usually none. Growth Rate – moderate.
Landscape Notes	Excellent as enclosure and foundation plant for large buildings or as large specimen. Attractive form and foliage; rarely produces flowers.

Laurus (law'rus)
    classical name
    of laurel

nobilis (no'bil-lis)
    noble, famous,
    renowned

LAUREL

Family Lauraceae

Zones	7, 8.
Size	Height 10-12 feet; spread 8-10 foot.
Form	Irregular and upright. Foliage – alternate, simple, 2-4 inches long, aromatic. Flower – inconspicuous. Fruit – fall; berries ½ inch diameter.
Texture	Medium to coarse.
Color	Foliage – bright green. Fruit – dark green becoming black.
Culture	Sun. Soil – good drainage; high fertility. Moisture – high. Pruning – none required but may be sheared to any desired form. Pest Problems – none. Growth Rate – moderate.
Landscape Notes	Ancient and famous plant. Dried leaves used as seasoning; essential for herb gardens. Grows well in tubs if pruned rigorously. Often used as screen or informal hedge. Grows well in Coastal Plain and Piedmont.

Ligustrum (ly-gus'trum)
   classical Latin name
   of privet

japonicum (ja-pon'i-kum)
   from Japan

JAPANESE PRIVET

Family Oleaceae

Zones	7,8.
Size	Height 6-10 feet; spread 5-6 feet.
Form	Erect with ovate head on short trunk. Foliage – opposite, simple, entire, to 4 inches long and rather leathery with veins on underside raised. Flower – May; 4-6 inch terminal racemes of small conspicuous blossoms with very strong odor. Fruit – fall; berry about ¼ inch long, racemose, conspicuous.
Texture	Coarse.
Color	Foliage – dark green. Flower – white. Fruit – blue-black.
Culture	Sun or shade. Soil – medium drainage; medium fertility. Moisture – medium. Pruning – none. Pest Problems – white flies and scale. Growth Rate – rapid.
Landscape Notes	Good for formal or informal hedge or shrub border. Adapted to adverse conditions of drought, heat, cold, and salt spray. Effective trained as topiary. Use in foundation plantings only for large structures and sites. Excellent background material.
Variety	'Lusterleaf' – large, thick leaves.

Ligustrum (ly-gus'trum)
 classical Latin name
 of privet

lucidum (lew'si-dum)
 bright or shining

TALL GLOSSY PRIVET

Family Oleaceae

Zones	7, 8.
Size	Height 8-12 feet; spread 5-10 feet.
Form	Spreading, irregular, and slightly horizontal. Foliage – opposite, simple, entire, to 6 inches long, and rather thin with veins on underside sunken. Flower – June; clusters 8-9 inches long. Fruit – fall; clusters of berries.
Texture	Coarse.
Color	Foliage – dark green. Flower – white. Fruit – dark purple-blue.
Culture	Sun or shade. Soil – medium drainage; medium fertility. Moisture – medium. Pruning – occasional corrective training for shape, avoid heavy pruning. Pest Problems – white flies and scale. Growth Rate – very rapid.
Landscape Notes	Does well in adverse conditions. Especially adapted to large extensive areas. Excellent as tall screen or windbreak. Mature specimens easily trimmed to multitrunk tree forms.
Variety	*nobilis* – branches strongly ascending.

Ligustrum (ly-gus'trum)
  classical Latin name
  of privet

vicaryi (vy-kare'ee-eye)
  named for
  Vicary Gibbs

VICARY GOLDEN PRIVET

Family Oleaceae

Zones	6, 7, 8.
Size	Height 8-10 feet; spread 6-9 feet.
Form	Upright oval. Foliage – opposite, simple, entire, 2 inches long. Flower – July; small racemes 3 inches long. Fruit – fall; berries.
Texture	Medium.
Color	Foliage – golden-yellow. Flower – white. Fruit – blue-black.
Culture	Sun. Soil – medium drainage; medium fertility. Moisture – medium. Pruning – none. Pest Problems – none. Growth Rate – moderate.
Landscape Notes	Excellent color constancy; no leaf scorch as in some variegated privets. May be used as specimen or in group plantings. Has hardiness of other privets. Good against dark background. Hybrid between *L. ovalifolium* 'Aureum' and *L. vulgare*.

Loropetalum (lor-o-pet'a-lum)
  Greek for strap and petal,
  in allusion to shape of
  petals

chinense (chi-nen'see)
  from China

LOROPETALUM

Family Hamamelidaceae

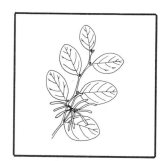

Zones	7,8.
Size	Height 6-10 feet; spread 8-9 feet.
Form	Irregular and rounded with horizontal twigs giving flat foliage effect. Foliage – alternate, entire, 1-2 inches long, oval, with rough surface. Flower – March; feathery petals 1 inch long. Fruit – summer; woody capsule.
Texture	Medium to fine.
Color	Foliage – dark green. Flower – white or cream. Fruit – brown.
Culture	Sun or part shade. Soil – good drainage; high fertility. Moisture – high. Pruning – none. Pest Problems – none. Growth Rate – rapid.
Landscape Notes	Showy flowers in early spring. Useful as screen, border, or foundation shrub; should be more widely planted. Excellent espaliered.

Magnolia (mag-no'li-a)
  named for Pierre Magnol

virginiana (vir-gin-i-a'na)
  from Virginia

SWEET BAY

Family Magnoliaceae

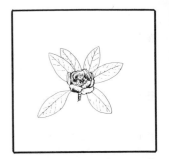

Zones	6, 7, 8.
Size	Height 10-12 feet; spread 8-10 feet.
Form	Rounded with irregular branching and open crown; in native areas, larger, more regular, and more dense. Foliage – alternate, simple, entire, 3-5 inches long, oblong and thick with slender petioles. Flower – early summer; terminal, like small magnolia, 2-3 inch diameter, very fragrant. Fruit – late summer or early fall; conelike, conspicuous. Bark – smooth.
Texture	Medium.
Color	Foliage – gray-green, white beneath. Flower – creamy-white. Fruit – red. Bark – yellow-gray, twig glaucous green.
Culture	Sun or part shade. Soil – low to medium drainage; high fertility. Moisture – high. Pruning – tolerant. Pest Problems – scale. Growth Rate – slow to moderate.
Landscape Notes	Native to coastal areas and sometimes reaches treelike proportions. Becomes deciduous farther north. Light and airy effect. Use against architectural or evergreen background. Not easy to transplant; move when actively beginning growth.

Michelia (me-chel'i-a)
   named for P.A. Micheli,
   Florentine botanist

figo (fy'go)
   unexplained

BANANA-SHRUB

Family Magnoliaceae

Zones	7, 8.
Size	Height 6-8 feet; spread 6-8 feet.
Form	Rounded, dense, and massive; rich and refined in character. Foliage – alternate, 3 inches long, narrow-oval. Flower – April through June; magnolia-type, 1½ inch diameter, fragrant.
Texture	Medium.
Color	Foliage – glossy dark green. Flower – yellowish-white, edged with maroon.
Culture	Sun or light shade. Soil – good drainage; medium fertility in sandy loam with high organic content. Moisture – medium. Pruning – none. Pest Problems – none. Growth Rate – slow.
Landscape Notes	Handsome foliage and pleasant banana fragrance from flowers in evening. Foliage may freeze in severe winters. Needs no care after established. Choice specimen plant for Coastal Plain. Often listed as *M. fuscata*.

Myrica (mir-i'ka)
 ancient Greek,
 possibly name
 for tamarisk

cerifera (se-rif'fer-ra)
 wax-bearing

WAX-MYRTLE

Family Myricaceae

Zones	7, 8.
Size	Height 10-12 feet; spread 4-6 feet.
Form	Irregular form. Foliage – alternate, 3 inches long, leathery, lanceolate to oblong-lanceolate, aromatic. Flower – early spring; inconspicuous. Fruit – late summer through winter; clusters of ⅛ inch globular berries covered with whitish resin; only on female plants.
Texture	Fine to medium.
Color	Foliage – yellow-green. Fruit – gray-green.
Culture	Sun or part shade. Soil – tolerant; medium drainage; medium to high fertility. Moisture – high. Pruning – none. Pest Problems – none. Growth Rate – moderate to rapid.
Landscape Notes	Will thrive in practically any situation. Good background material; combines well with junipers. May be used in borders or trimmed to tree-form for planter boxes. Provides good foliage texture and color contrast in borders. Plentiful in Carolina coastal area. Useful on coast but will not tolerate direct exposure to salt spray. Not for mountain areas. Fruit attracts birds.

Myrtus (mir'tus)
  ancient Greek name

communis (cahm-myoon'iss)
  growing in common or
  community

MYRTLE

Family Myrtaceae

Zone	8.
Size	Height 5-10 feet; spread 4-7 feet.
Form	Open and upright. Foliage – opposite, entire, 2 inches long, aromatic. Flower – spring; ¾ inch diameter in axils; stamens prominent. Fruit – fall; berry ½ inch long.
Texture	Fine.
Color	Foliage – dark green. Flower – clear white. Fruit – blue-black.
Culture	Sun. Soil – tolerant. Moisture – medium. Pruning – withstands shearing. Pest Problems – mites, scales, and mushroom root rot. Growth Rate – moderate.
Landscape Notes	Excellent specimen or for sheared or natural hedges. Useful for foundation plantings for large buildings. Transplants poorly and is difficult to establish.
Variety	'Compacta' – to 3 feet in height with compact, rounded form. Excellent for edging and small specimen. Slightly more cold hardy than species.

Nerium (neer'i-um)
Greek name of
oleander

oleander (oh-lee-ann'der)
with leaves like olive

OLEANDER

Family Apocynaceae

Zone	8.
Size	Height 7-10 feet; spread 6-9 feet.
Form	Upright and rounded. Foliage – in whorls of 3, rarely in 4's or opposite, 5-7 inches long, narrow-oblong, leathery. Flower – spring and summer; 3 inch diameter in terminal cymes, fragrant, single or double. Fruit – summer; pods 7 inches long.
Texture	Fine to medium.
Color	Foliage – gray-green. Flower – red, pink, yellow, or white. Fruit – green turning black.
Culture	Sun. Soil – very tolerant; medium drainage; medium fertility. Moisture – medium to low. Pruning – remove old wood occasionally. Pest Problems – scale and mealybugs. Growth Rate – rapid.
Landscape Notes	Grows very well in coastal areas with little care. Showy clusters of fragrant flowers all summer; excellent as specimen and in shrub borders. Excellent tub or container plant. High salt and wind tolerance. All parts of plant very toxic. Hardy in zone 7 with heavy protection in winter.
Varieties	'Cardinal' – red flowers. 'Compte Barthelemy' – double red flowers. 'Mrs. Roeding' – double pink flowers.

Osmanthus (oz-man'thus)
Greek for fragrance
and flower

fortunei (for-too'nee-i) .
named for Robert Fortune

FORTUNE TEA OLIVE

Family Oleaceae

Zones	7, 8.
Size	Height 9-12 feet; spread 5-7 feet.
Form	Rounded and compact. Foliage – opposite, 4 inches long, spiny. Flower – fall; very small and fragrant axillary clusters.
Texture	Medium.
Color	Foliage – dark green. Flower – white.
Culture	Sun. Soil – tolerant; medium drainage; medium fertility. Moisture – medium. Pruning – none. Pest Problems – none. Growth Rate – moderate.
Landscape Notes	Excellent in large borders and screens or as clipped hedge. May be used as formal specimen. Hybrid of *O. fragrans* and *O. heterophyllus*.

Osmanthus (oz-man'thus)
   Greek for fragrance
   and flower

fragrans (fray'granz)
   fragrant

FRAGRANT TEA OLIVE

Family Oleaceae

Zones	7, 8.
Size	Height 10-12 feet; spread 10-14 feet.
Form	Upright and rounded. Foliage – opposite, to 4 inches long, no spines. Flower – October through January; small, very sweet fragrance.
Texture	Medium.
Color	Foliage – deep green. Flower – white.
Culture	Sun or part shade. Soil – tolerant; medium drainage; medium fertility. Moisture – medium to high. Pruning – intolerant of shearing. Pest Problems – none. Growth Rate – moderate.
Landscape Notes	May become treelike in Coastal Plain. Use as large specimen near porch or walkway where delightful fragrance can be appreciated. Less hardy than *O. fortunei* and may be killed to ground in Western Carolina in severe winters.

Osmanthus (oz-man'thus)
  Greek for fragrance
  and flower

heterophyllus (het-er-o-fill'us)
  with variously shaped leaves

HOLLY OSMANTHUS

Family Oleaceae

Zones	6, 7, 8.
Size	Height 6-10 feet; spread 3-5 feet.
Form	Upright with irregular shape. Foliage – opposite, to 2½ inches long, usually spiny. Flower – July and August; small, very fragrant.
Texture	Medium.
Color	Foliage – deep green. Flower – white.
Culture	Sun or part shade. Soil – tolerant; medium drainage; medium fertility. Moisture – medium. Pruning – none. Pest Problems – none. Growth Rate – moderate.
Landscape Notes	May be used as formal specimen or hedge. Useful as background planting. Varieties with small leaves occasionally offered. Formerly listed as *O. ilicifolius*.

Osmanthus (oz-man'thus)
Greek for fragrance
and flower

heterophyllus (het-er-o-fill'us)
with variously shaped leaves

rotundifolius (ro-tun-di-fol'li-us)
round-leaved

CURLYLEAF TEA OLIVE

Family Oleaceae

Zones	6, 7, 8.
Size	Height 6-10 feet; spread to 6 feet.
Form	Rounded, spreading, and irregular. Foliage – opposite, about 1 inch long, wavy margins, thick and leathery. Flower – fall; inconspicuous, very fragrant.
Texture	Medium.
Color	Foliage – dark green. Flower – white.
Culture	Sun or part shade. Soil – tolerant; prefers loam. Moisture – medium. Pruning – shape. Pest Problems – none. Growth Rate – moderate to rapid.
Landscape Notes	Excellent holly substitute. May be used as irregular hedge, specimen, or accent plant.

Photinia (fo-tin'i-a)
　　Greek for shining,
　　in allusion to glossy
　　leaves

fraseri (fra'ser-i)
　　named for John
　　Fraser, English
　　botanist

FRASER PHOTINIA

Family Rosaceae

Zones	7,8.
Size	Height 7-12 feet; spread 5-8 feet.
Form	Upright, slightly rounded. Foliage – alternate, 5 inches long, few or no teeth on margins. Flower – April; small clusters. Fruit – fall; berrylike.
Texture	Coarse.
Color	Foliage – medium to dark green; copper-red with bright red stems when immature. Flower – white. Fruit – red.
Culture	Sun. Soil – medium drainage; medium fertility with high organic content. Moisture – medium. Pruning – very tolerant. Pest Problems – none. Growth Rate – rapid.
Landscape Notes	Hybrid between *P. glabra* and *P. serrulata* having good characteristics of both parents. Resistant to mildew which disfigures *P. serrulata*. Best used for hedge in full sun or where color harmonizies.

Photinia (fo-tin'i-a)
Greek for shining,
in allusion to glossy
leaves

glabra (glay'bra)
smooth

RED PHOTINIA

Family Rosaceae

Zones	7, 8.
Size	Height 6-10 feet; spread 4-5 feet.
Form	Upright, rather loose. Foliage – alternate, to 3 inches long, smooth edged or very finely toothed. Flower – summer; flat 4 inch clusters. Fruit – fall; fleshy peasize berries in clusters.
Texture	Medium.
Color	Foliage – young leaves, bright red; mature leaves, medium dull green. Flower – white. Fruit – red.
Culture	Sun. Soil – medium drainage; medium fertility with high organic content. Moisture – medium. Pruning – very tolerant. Pest Problems – none. Growth Rate – rapid.
Landscape Notes	Best used for hedges in full sun or where color harmonizes. Avoid placing against red brick walls.

Photina (fo-tin'i-a)
    Greek for shining,
    in allusion to glossy
    leaves

serrulata (sir-roo-lay'ta)
    serrulate

CHINESE PHOTINIA

Family Rosaceae

Zones	7,8.
Size	Height 7-12 feet; spread 5-12 feet.
Form	Broadly oval, occasionally becoming multiple trunked small tree. Foliage – alternate, to 8 inches long, usually with serrate edge. Flower – May; 6 inch heads on terminal growth. Fruit – late summer; clusters of berries ¼ inch in diameter.
Texture	Coarse.
Color	Foliage – green with slight maroon coloration in early spring, young foliage coppery-red. Flower – white. Fruit – red.
Culture	Sun. Soil – good drainage; medium fertility with high organic content. Moisture – low to medium. Pruning – very tolerant. Pest Problems – scale, European fruit-tip moth, leaf spot, and mildew. Growth Rate – rapid.
Landscape Notes	Limited landscape use because of color and susceptibility to mildew. Large specimen or accent plant for unlimited areas requiring mass. Container grown stock easier to transplant.

Pittosporum (pit-toss'por-rum)
     Greek for pitch and seed
     referring to resinous
     coating of seeds

tobira (toe-by'ra)
     native Japanese name

PITTOSPORUM
Family Pittosporaceae

Zone	8.
Size	Height 8-10 feet; spread 6-9 feet.
Form	Stiff bushy growth with interesting branching habit. Foliage – alternate, blunt, leathery, thick, to 4 inches long. Flower – April through May; about 1 inch diameter in clusters; fragrance similar to orange blossoms. Fruit – October and November; 4-angled capsule.
Texture	Medium.
Color	Foliage – dark green. Flower – creamy-white. Fruit – brown.
Culture	Sun in Coastal Plains, requires some shade in Piedmont. Soil – good drainage; medium fertility. Moisture – medium. Pruning – may be sheared if started when young. Pest Problems – cottony cushion scale. Growth Rate – moderate to rapid.
Landscape Notes	Excellent as specimen plant or for natural or clipped hedges, screens, and planter boxes. Very popular for beach landscaping.
Variety	'White Spot' – attractive white and green leaves; smaller than the species; less hardy.

Podocarpus (po-do-kar'pus)
   Greek for foot and fruit,
   in allusion to prominent
   stalk of fruit

macrophyllus (mak-ro-fil'lus)
   large leaved

maki (mac'e)
   Japanese name

PODOCARPUS

Family Podocarpaceae

Zones	7, 8.
Size	Height 8-10 feet; spread 3-5 feet.
Form	Pyramidal branches upright and dense. Foliage – alternate, simple, 2-3 inches long and ⅓ inch wide, with distinct midrib. Flower – catkins. Fruit – ⅓-½ inch long.
Texture	Fine.
Color	Foliage – lustrous medium green above, paler beneath. Fruit – greenish or purplish.
Culture	Sun or shade. Soil – medium drainage; medium fertility in sandy loam. Moisture – medium to high. Pruning – easily clipped to form many different and interesting shapes. Pest Problems – none. Growth Rate – slow.
Landscape Notes	Excellent specimen, hedge, or screening material for large or small gardens. Withstands city conditions. Useful to contrast foliage and form in mixed plantings and for espalier. Particularly good for Coastal Plains; tips sometimes winter-kill in Piedmont areas.

Prunus (proo'nuss)
    classical Latin
    name of plum

laurocerasus (law-ro-se'ra-sus)
    classical name of laurel

ENGLISH LAUREL

Family Rosaceae

Zones	6, 7, 8.
Size	Height 10-12 feet; spread 8-11 feet.
Form	Upright, semiconical to slightly open. Foliage – alternate, 4-6 inches long. Flower – spring; racemes 2-5 inches long. Fruit – inconspicuous.
Texture	Medium to coarse.
Color	Foliage – glossy light green. Flower – white.
Culture	Sun or shade. Soil – good drainage; medium fertility with high organic content. Moisture – medium. Pruning – sometimes needs training for central leader; old plants occasionally need severe renovation. Pest Problems – wood borers and leaf spot. Growth Rate – moderate.
Landscape Notes	Sometimes has scorched foliage appearance, especially in winter. Often sheds foliage when transplanted. May be used for tall hedges, windbreaks, or foundation planting for large buildings.
Variety	'Otto Luyken' – broad spreading dwarf. Less than 3 feet in height and 5-7 feet wide when fully mature.

Pyracantha (py-ra-kan'tha)
   from Greek for fire
   and thorn

koidzumi (koyd-zoo'my)
   native name in Formosa

FORMOSA FIRETHORN

Family Rosaceae

Zones	7, 8.
Size	Height 6-10 feet; spread 6-10 feet.
Form	Dense and irregularly spreading. Foliage – alternate, 1-2 inches long, wedge-shaped with notch at tip, pubescent beneath. Flower – May; ¼ inch diameter in 1 inch clusters, fragrant. Fruit – fall; ¼ inch berries.
Texture	Medium.
Color	Foliage – grayish-green. Flower – white. Fruit – orange to dark red.
Culture	Sun or part shade. Soil – good drainage; medium fertility. Moisture – medium. Pruning – prevent legginess and train. Pest Problems – fire blight, lacebug, and scale. Growth Rate – rapid.
Landscape Notes	Heavy clusters of bright red fruit in fall and winter. Hardy through Coastal Plain and warmer parts of Piedmont. Interesting as specimen, border, or screen plant. Often seen espaliered or trained on trellis.
Varieties	'San Jose' – widely spreading form. 'Santa Cruz' – prostrate form; red berries. 'Victory' – dark red berries; very showy.

Viburnum (vy-bur'num)
  classical Latin name
  of wayfaring tree

rhytidophyllum (rit-i-do-fill'um)
  wrinkle-leaved

LEATHERLEAF VIBURNUM

Family Caprifoliaceae

Zones	6, 7, 8.
Size	Height 6-10 feet; spread 5-7 feet.
Form	Upright and inclined to legginess. Foliage – opposite, entire, 3-7 inches long with prominent veins beneath. Flower – May; cymes 4-8 inch diameter. Fruit – autumn; berries ¼-½ inch long.
Texture	Coarse.
Color	Foliage – lustrous dark green above, rusty tomentose beneath. Flower – yellowish-white, not attractive. Fruit – red turning black.
Culture	Shade or part shade with shelter from excessive wind exposure. Soil – medium drainage; medium fertility. Moisture – medium. Pruning – none. Pest Problems – none. Growth Rate – moderate.
Landscape Notes	Dignified shrub of architectural character; excellent foliage and fruit. Used as specimen and foundation plant especially for narrow wall spots. Grown for interesting form and foliage texture.
Variety	*roseum* – pink flower buds.

Viburnum (vy-bur'num)
  classical Latin name
  of wayfaring tree

tinus (ty'nus)
  pre-Linnean name
  for laurestinus

LAURESTINUS VIBURNUM

Family Caprifoliaceae

Zones	7,8.
Size	Height 10-12 feet; spread 10-12 feet.
Form	Globe-shaped. Foliage – opposite, 2-3 inches long, shiny above, pubescent beneath on veins. Flower – early spring; fragrant cyme 2-3 inch diameter. Fruit – summer; ovoid, partially dry.
Texture	Coarse.
Color	Foliage – dark green. Flower – white to pinkish. Fruit – blue-black.
Culture	Sun or part shade. Soil – tolerant; medium drainage; medium fertility. Moisture – medium to high. Pruning – none. Pest Problems – mildew. Growth Rate – moderate.
Landscape Notes	Valuable evergreen for barrier, specimen, clipped or unclipped hedge. Bears luxuriant masses of leaves. Avoid watering in fall or planting on very fertile soils. Good background material.
Variety	'Lucidum' – large flower clusters.

Yucca (yuk′ka)
    Latinized version of
    Spanish vernacular for
    some other desert plant

aloifolia (alo-i-fol′ia)
    with leaves like aloe

SPANISH-BAYONET

Family Liliaceae

Zone	8.
Size	Height 6-15 feet; spread 4-5 feet.
Form	Trunk tall, usually leaning, sometimes branched. Bottom leaves die off as trunk lengthens. Foliage – stiff and pointed, 2-2½ feet long, 2 inches wide with toothed margins. Flower – early summer; waxy, 4 inches wide in clusters 2 feet long, opening and fragrant at night. Fruit – October through December; 3½ inches long.
Texture	Coarse.
Color	Foliage – dark green. Flower – white, often tinged with purple. Fruit – purplish-black.
Culture	Sun or part shade. Soil – good drainage; low fertility; prefers sandy loam. Moisture – low. Pruning – remove dead or damaged leaves. Pest Problems – none. Growth Rate – moderate.
Landscape Notes	Excellent texture or form contrast against architectural features. Effective massed in large areas. May be used in city gardens or in protected beach plantings. Combines well with santolina.
Variety	*draconis* – trunk branched, leaves more flexible and recurved, not as rigid as species.

SHRUBS 6-12 FEET — DECIDUOUS

Azalea (a-zay'lee-a)
    showy shrubs, botanically
    Rhododendrons

calendulacea (ka-len-dew-lay'see-a)
    like marigold in its
    brilliant color

FLAME AZALEA

Family Ericaceae

Zones	6, 7, 8.
Size	Height 8-12 feet; spread 5-8 feet.
Form	Loosely open with broad spreading top. Foliage – midspring to midfall; alternate, entire, 1½-3½ inches long. Flower – early May with developing leaves; 2 inches wide in large clusters, very showy, glandular pubescent outside.
Texture	Medium.
Color	Foliage – light green. Flower – yellow, orange, and orange-red.
Culture	Sun to part shade; does not flower as profusely when shaded. Soil – medium drainage; medium fertility; slightly acid with 6 inch mulch of leaves or bark. Moisture – high. Pruning – tolerant. Pest Problems – usually none. Growth Rate – moderate.
Landscape Notes	Handsome and showy native azalea. Best in woodland plantings. Good fall color. Transplants easily when dormant. Grows wild through mountainous sections. Correct botanical name is *Rhododendron calendulaceum*.

Azalea (a-zay'lee-a)
  showy shrubs, botanically
  Rhododendrons

hybrida (hy'brid-a)
  hybrid

'Exbury' (ecks'berry)
  named for Exbury,
  Southhampton, England

EXBURY HYBRID AZALEA

Family Ericaceae

Zones	6, 7, 8.
Size	Height 6-8 feet; spread 5-7 feet.
Form	Upright and loose. Foliage – alternate, simple, entire, ½ inch wide, 2½ inches long, lanceolate. Flower – mid-April and May; 2-3 inches wide, mostly single, 6-18 in cluster.
Texture	Medium.
Color	Foliage – light green. Flower – white, cream, pink, orange, red, and intermediate colors, usually with gold blothes.
Culture	Part shade. Soil – good drainage; medium to high fertility with humus added. Moisture – high. Pruning – tolerant; shape and remove dead flowers and dead wood. Pest Problems – none. Growth Rate – moderate.
Landscape Notes	Excellent for naturalizing or in mass for color accent in spring. Effective in combination with evergreen azaleas and camellias. Often called Rothschild Azalea.

Azalea (a-zay'lee-a)
   showy shrubs, botanically
   Rhododendrons

nudiflora (new-di-flo'ra)
   flowers before leaves

PINXTERBLOOM AZALEA

Family Ericaceae

Zones	6, 7, 8.
Size	Height 5-8 feet; spread 2-6 feet.
Form	Usually low with spreading branches. Foliage – early spring to late fall; alternate, entire, 1½ - 3 inches long, crowded toward end of branches. Flower – mid-April; 1½ inches wide in large clusters, fragrant, corolla hairy.
Texture	Medium.
Color	Foliage – bright green above and downy, paler beneath. Flower – pink to white.
Culture	Part shade. Soil – very good drainage; medium fertility; slightly acid. Moisture – high. Pruning – tolerant. Pest Problems – usually none. Growth Rate – slow.
Landscape Notes	Native to southeastern areas. Self layering. Transplants easily when dormant. Useful in masses for naturalistic areas. Correct botanical name is *Rhododendron nudiflorum*.

Buddleia (bud-lee'a)
    named for Adam Buddle

davidii (da'vid-eye)
    named for Armand David

BUTTERFLY-BUSH

Family Loganiaceae

Zones	6, 7, 8.
Size	Height 5-8 feet; spread 3-6 feet.
Form	Open, irregular, and rambling with arching branches. Foliage – late spring to very late fall; opposite, 6-9 inches long. Flower – July and August; spikes 5-12 inches long, fragrant, attracting butterflies. Fruit – late fall; 2-celled capsules.
Texture	Coarse.
Color	Foliage – dull green. Flower – white, pink, red, or purple. Fruit – brownish-green.
Culture	Sun. Soil – good drainage; high fertility. Moisture – low. Pruning – cut to ground in fall. Pest Problems – nematodes. Growth Rate – rapid after established.
Landscape Notes	Valued for summer flowering and usually treated as perennial. Useful scattered through large shrub borders or as accent for flower beds.
Varieties	'Charming' – pink flowers in panicles 1-2 feet long. 'Dubonnet' – dark purple flowers. 'Empire Blue' – deep blue flowers in panicles ½-1 foot long. 'White Bouquet' – white flowers.

Calycanthus (kal-ee-kan'thus)
   Greek for calyx and flower,
   referring to colored calyx

floridus (flo'ri-dus)
   freely flowering

SWEETSHRUB

Family Calycanthaceae

Zones	6,7,8.
Size	Height 6-9 feet; spread 5-8 feet.
Form	Coarse, rounded, often straggling and open when mature. Foliage – early spring to early fall; opposite, to 6 inches long, aromatic when crushed. Flower – mid-April after leaves; 1½ inches wide, strawberry odor. Fruit – midsummer, long persistent; fig-shaped capsule, fragrant when crushed.
Texture	Rather coarse.
Color	Foliage – yellow-green; fall, yellow. Flower – dark reddish-brown. Fruit – tan-brown.
Culture	Sun or shade. Soil – tolerant; medium drainage; medium fertility. Moisture – medium. Pruning – occasional thinning and removing of dead wood. Pest Problems – none. Growth Rate – moderate.
Landscape Notes	Native to southeastern areas. Valued for fragrance of flowers and fruit; useful in unclipped borders and moist areas. Easily transplanted.

Chimonanthus (ky-mo-nan'thus)
Greek for snow and flower

praecox (pre'koks)
precocious, very early

WINTERSWEET

Family Calycanthaceae

Zones	6, 7, 8.
Size	Height 10-15 feet; spread 10 feet or more.
Form	Loose and upright. Foliage – opposite, 3-6 inches long. Flower – December on leafless branches, continues all winter; about 1 inch diameter, very fragrant.
Texture	Coarse.
Color	Foliage – lustrous rich green above, glabrous beneath; fall, clear yellow. Flower – yellow striped with purplish-brown.
Culture	Sun to part shade. Soil – tolerant; good drainage; medium fertility. Moisture – medium. Pruning – remove old wood occasionally. Pest Problems – none. Growth Rate – slow.
Landscape Notes	Valuable for fragrant flowering and fall color in screens and borders. Flowering branches useful for floral arrangements.

Chionanthus (ki-o-nan'thus)
Greek for snow and flower

virginicus (vir-gin'i-cus)
from Virginia

FRINGETREE

Family Oleaceae

Zones	6, 7, 8.
Size	Height 10-12 feet; spread 8-10 feet.
Form	Large shrub or small tree with somewhat stiff, spreading branches, round-topped, usually taller than broad. Foliage – very late to leaf out in spring, drops in midfall; opposite, entire, to 8 inches long. Flower – early May; pendulous, panicles often unisexual, 1 inch long in clusters to 8 inches long. Fruit – late summer and early fall; drupes.
Texture	Coarse.
Color	Foliage – bright green; fall, yellow. Flower – white. Fruit – dark blue.
Culture	Sun. Soil – medium drainage; medium fertility in sandy loam. Moisture – medium. Pruning – thin occasionally to stimulate new growth. Pest Problems – none. Growth Rate – slow.
Landscape Notes	Valued for fragrance and beauty of flowers; used generally as specimen; good in cities, will endure smoke and dust. Difficult to transplant, very slow to grow roots. Flowers on male plants larger and more showy, fruit only on female plants. May be trained as small tree.

Cortaderia (kor-ta-deer'ia)
   from *Cortadero*, native
   name in Argentina

selloana (sel-lo-a'na)
   named for Friedrich Sello,
   German traveler in
   South America

PAMPAS GRASS

Famjly Poaceae

Zones	7, 8.
Size	Height 3-10 feet; spread to 6 feet.
Form	Perennial grass; upright and open to upright-narrow. Foliage – 3-10 feet arching to ground, ¾ inch wide. Flower – September to late October; panicles 20-36 inches long; silky and hairy.
Texture	Fine.
Color	Foliage – medium green; fall, beige. Flower – white.
Culture	Sun or part shade. Soil – good drainage; medium to high fertility. Moisture – low to medium. Pruning – trim to ground yearly for new growth. Pest Problems – none. Growth Rate – rapid.
Landscape Notes	Excellent as specimen in larger areas with flowers and foliage giving striking effect. Limited in use by large size. Use female plants for best flower display.

Cotoneaster (ko-to'nee-as-ter)
Greek meaning like quince

salicifolia (sal-is-i-fo'li-a)
leaves like willow

floccosa (flok-ko'sa)
woolly

WILLOWLEAF COTONEASTER

Family Rosaceae

Zones	6, 7, 8.
Size	Height 7-12 feet; spread 7-12 feet.
Form	Upright branches arching gracefully. Foliage – alternate, narrow, 2-4 inches long with red veins, woolly beneath. Flower – spring; small clusters. Fruit – fall and winter; clusters of ¼ inch berries.
Texture	Medium.
Color	Foliage – dark green; fall, purple-red. Flower – white. Fruit – red.
Culture	Part shade. Soil – good drainage; medium to low fertility. Moisture – medium to high. Pruning – none. Pest Problems – fire blight, scale, and lacebug. Growth Rate – slow.
Landscape Notes	Semievergreen in cool areas. Outstanding in form, foliage, and fruit. For parks or large gardens as specimen or background.

Cytisus (sit'i-sus)
Greek for some cloverlike
plant, in allusion to
3 leaflets

scoparius (sko-pair'i-us)
broomlike

SCOTCH BROOM

Family Fabaceae

Zones	6, 7, 8.
Size	Height 5-7 feet; spread 3-5 feet.
Form	Upright, fan-shaped, fairly open. Foliage – alternate, compound, usually 3 leaflets ⅓ inch long. Flower – late April and early May; pealike, 1 inch long. Fruit – summer; pod 1½-2 inches long. Twigs – ridged.
Texture	Fine.
Color	Foliage – medium green. Flower – yellow or pink. Twigs – green.
Culture	Sun to part shade. Soil – very tolerant; medium to good drainage; medium fertility. Moisture – medium. Pruning – remove dead wood. Pest Problems – none. Growth Rate – rapid.
Landscape Notes	Form derived from vertical twig growth rather than foliage effect; somewhat unpredictable in survival. Numerous seedlings replace old plants. Has become naturalized in spots all over Southeastern United States. Will grow on clay banks.
Varieties	'Burkwoodii' – upright in habit; crimson flowers. 'Pink Beauty' – pink flowers. 'St. Mary's' – cream white flowers.

Deutzia (doot'zi-a)
  named for Johann
  van der Deutz

scabra (skay'bra)
  rough

PRIDE OF ROCHESTER

Family Saxifragaceae

Zones	6, 7, 8.
Size	Height 6-10 feet; spread 4-8 feet.
Form	Tall and erect. Foliage – late spring to midfall; opposite, simple, 2 inches long, ovate, covered with minute, roughish hairs like sandpaper. Flower – late May; 1 inch diameter, double. Fruit – early fall, persisting through winter; capsules.
Texture	Coarse.
Color	Foliage – dull green; fall, yellow. Flower – white or tinged pink. Fruit – brown. Bark – dark brown, golden brown inner bark.
Culture	Sun or part shade. Soil – tolerant; good drainage; medium fertility. Moisture – medium. Pruning – not tolerant but needs occasional thinning and removal of dead wood. Pest Problems – aphids. Growth Rate – moderate.
Landscape Notes	Handsome mass useful in shrub borders or as specimen. Very showy in flower. Useful as background or accent for flower beds.

Euonymus (you-on'i-mus)
  hardy shrubs and vines

alatus (a-lay'tus)
  winged

WINGED EUONYMUS

Family Celastraceae

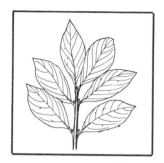

Zones	6, 7, 8.
Size	Height 5-8 feet; spread 3-5 feet.
Form	Upright with horizontal branching and rugged twig structures. Foliage – opposite, 1½-3 inches long. Flower – inconspicuous. Fruit- fall, persisting; capsules opening to expose brightly colored interior.
Texture	Medium.
Color	Foliage – green, slightly mottled; fall, scarlet. Fruit – pink to scarlet. Twigs – green with corky ridges.
Culture	Sun to part shade. Soil – medium drainage; medium fertility. Mois- ture – medium to high. Pruning – shape and maintain density. Pest Problems – scale. Growth Rate – moderate.
Landscape Notes	Excellent for parks or industrial sites. Flamboyant coloring and rank growth limit use to large-scale properties. Grown for fall color and interesting twig structure in winter.
Variety	'Compactus' – dwarf form to 4 feet tall.

Euonymus (you-on'i-mus)
   hardy shrubs and vines

americanus (a-me-ri-cay'nus)
   from North or
   South America

STRAWBERRY-BUSH

Family Celastraceae

Zones	6, 7.
Size	Height 7-8 feet; spread 6-7 feet.
Form	Spreading and irregular with rounded crown and sparse upright or trailing branches. Foliage – opposite, 1-3 inches long. Flower – May to June; ½ inch wide, inconspicuous. Fruit – early fall; capsules 1-2 inches wide with warty covering that cracks to expose seeds, pendulous.
Texture	Medium.
Color	Foliage – dark green; fall, bright red. Flower – reddish-green. Fruit – orange-red covering with scarlet seeds inside. Stem – green.
Culture	Shade. Soil – good drainage; medium fertility. Moisture – medium. Pruning – shape. Pest Problems – euonymus scale and crown gall. Growth Rate – rapid if in fertile soil.
Landscape Notes	Useful of naturalizing. Fall color and fruit interesting. Gives striking effect massed with water in foreground.

Exochorda (ecks-o-kor'da)
Greek external cord,
referring to internal
structures in carpels

racemosa (ra-see-mo'sa)
flowers in racemes

PEARLBUSH

Family Rosaceae

Zones	6, 7, 8.
Size	Height 10-12 feet; spread 8-10 feet.
Form	Loose and irregular in growth, becoming open and picturesque; may become straggly; occasionally treelike. Foliage – mid-spring to midfall; alternate, simple, toothed, thin, 2 inches long, oblong-ovate. Flower – early April with leaves; buds pearllike; loose terminal racemes, 2 inch diameter, odorless. Fruit – early summer; 5-lobed capsules.
Texture	Medium.
Color	Foliage – bluish-green. Flower – buds white, flowers white with green centers. Fruit – brown.
Culture	Sun or part shade. Soil – good drainage; medium fertility, slightly acid. Moisture – medium. Pruning – shape and maintain compact form. Pest Problems – none. Growth Rate – moderate.
Landscape Notes	Delicate appearance in bloom; attractive foliage. Grows leggy with age, requiring facer shrubs. Valuable as light mass or specimen for large areas. Sometimes difficult to transplant.

Forsythia (for-sith'i-a)
   named for William Forsyth

intermedia (in-ter-mee'di-a)
   intermediate

BORDER FORSYTHIA

Family Oleaceae

Zones	6, 7, 8.
Size	Height 8-10 feet; spread 7-10 feet.
Form	Erect with arching branches. Foliage – midspring to late fall; opposite, 3-5 inches long, often 3-parted. Flower – early March, **before** leaves; 1¼ inches long, bell-like, profusely produced in clusters. Fruit – late summer, more or less persisting; dry capsule.
Texture	Medium.
Color	Foliage – deep green. Flower – yellow. Fruit – brown.
Culture	Sun. Soil – tolerant; good drainage; medium fertility. Moisture – low to medium. Pruning – tolerant (prune after flowering); thin and renew occasionally, cutting 3-year old wood at ground. Pest Problems – none. Growth Rate – rapid.
Landscape Notes	Good foliage mass but most beautiful in flower; useful as large accent, dense mass or screen, and in border with spring bulbs. Withstands city conditions. Transplants well, roots quickly. Hybrid between *F. suspensa* and *F. viridissima*.
Varieties	'Beatrix Farrand' – vivid yellow flowers, 2 inch diameter. 'Lynwood Gold' – deep yellow flowers; upright in habit.

Hamamelis (ham-am-ee'lis)
    Greek for together and apple;
    flowers and fruit are produced
    at same time

virginiana (vir-gin-i-a'na)
    from Virginia

COMMON WITCH-HAZEL

Family Hamamelidaceae

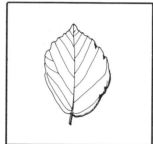

Zones	6, 7.
Size	Height 8-15 feet; spread 7-14 feet.
Form	Round to vase-shaped with open horizontal branching. Foliage – alternate, 4-6 inches long. Flower – October to November; ¾ inch wide with 4 petals. fragrant. Fruit – December; dry capsule.
Texture	Coarse.
Color	Foliage – medium green; fall, golden yellow. Flower – bright yellow. Fruit – brown with black seeds.
Culture	Sun to shade. Soil – medium drainage; low to medium fertility with humus added. Moisture – medium to high. Pruning – none. Pest Problems – none. Growth Rate – moderate to rapid.
Landscape Notes	Excellent for naturalizing in shady areas. Blooms after leaves have fallen. Most useful for large estates and parks.

Hydrangea (hy-dran'ji-a)
  hardy shrubs, vines

paniculata (pan-ick-kew-lay'ta)
  compound raceme

'Grandiflora' (gran-di-flo'ra)
  large or showy flowered

PEEGEE HYDRANGEA

Family Saxifragaceae

Zones	6, 7, 8.
Size	Height 8-20 feet; spread 6-8 feet.
Form	Rounded, loose; occasionally treelike. Foliage – opposite, oval, 3-5 inches long with toothed margin. Flower – July; small in pyramidal clusters to 12 inches; most florets sterile. Fruit – usually none.
Texture	Coarse.
Color	Foliage – medium green. Flower – white, turning pink at maturity.
Culture	Part shade. Soil – tolerant. Moisture – medium. Pruning – cut back old wood in late winter or early spring to encourage shrubby form and flowering. Pest Problems – powdery mildew. Growth Rate – rapid.
Landscape Notes	Grows well in seaside gardens; tolerant of city conditions. May be trimmed to form small tree.

Kolkwitzia (kolk-wit'zi-a)
  named for Richard Kolkwitz

amabilis (a-mab'i-lis)
  lovely

BEAUTYBUSH

Family Caprifoliaceae

Zones	6, 7, 8.
Size	Height 6-7 feet; spread 6-8 feet.
Form	Erect, vase-shaped, rather dense, broader than tall, branching to ground. Foliage – midspring to midfall; opposite, 2-3 inches long, ovate, shallowly toothed. Flower – early May; on short growth of current season; ½ inch long, in profuse clusters. Fruit – summer; dry capsule.
Texture	Medium to fine.
Color	Foliage – gray-green; fall, reddish. Flower – pink with yellow throat. Fruit – brown.
Culture	Sun. Soil – tolerant; good drainage; medium fertility. Moisture – medium. Pruning – during first years pinch back to thicken growth. Pest Problems – none. Growth Rate – slow.
Landscape Notes	Good mass when properly maintained, otherwise loose and open; useful in shrub borders. Transplants poorly, slow to reestablish.

Lonicera (lon-iss'er-ra)
  honeysuckles

fragrantissima (fray-gran-tiss'i-ma)
  very fragrant

WINTER HONEYSUCKLE

Family Caprifoliaceae

Zones	6, 7, 8.
Size	Height 6-8 feet; spread 6-8 feet.
Form	Globe-shaped with arching branches; medium to heavy density. Foliage – opposite, simple, entire, 1-2 inches long, thick, leathery. Flower – January to early March; ½ inch long, bell-shaped, fragrant. Fruit – summer; small berry, inconspicuous.
Texture	Medium.
Color	Foliage – blue-green. Flower – creamy white. Fruit – red.
Culture	Sun or shade. Soil – medium drainage; medium fertility. Moisture – medium. Pruning – cut oldest branches to ground every 2 or 3 years for density and shape. Pest Problems – none. Growth Rate – rapid.
Landscape Notes	Very good for light screening and background. Flowers extremely fragrant. Easily transplanted.

Magnolia (mag-no'li-a)
   named for Pierre Magnol

stellata (stell-lay'ta)
   starlike

STAR MAGNOLIA

Family Magnoliaceae

Zones	6, 7, 8.
Size	Height 10-12 feet; spread 8-10 feet.
Form	Broad and rounded mass becoming treelike with age. Foliage – late spring to early fall; alternate, simple, entire, leathery, 2-4 inches long. Flower – March before leaves appear; 3 inch diameter, fragrant. Fruit – autumn, not very persistent; 2 inches long, podlike, colorful. Bark – smooth with buds and branches densely hairy.
Texture	Coarse.
Color	Foliage – deep green; fall, bronze. Flower – white. Fruit – rosy-red.
Culture	Sun; cannot compete with tree roots and will not tolerate shade. Soil – good drainage; high fertility. Moisture – high. Pruning – not tolerant. Pest Problems – scale. Growth Rate – slow.
Landscape Notes	Very handsome specimen shrub for lawns and gardens; best with darker background to set off bloom. Blooms may be killed by frost. Difficult to transplant; move only when in active growth. Water through summer after moving.
Variety	*rosea* – pink flower buds, flower 4 inch diameter, pale pink fading to white. Pink Star Magnolia.

Malus (may'lus)
ancient Latin
name for apple

sargentii (sar-jent'ee-eye)
named for C.S. Sargent,
first director of
Arnold Arboretum

SARGENT CRAB APPLE

Family Rosaceae

Zones	6, 7.
Size	Height 6-8 feet; spread 8-10 feet.
Form	Irregularly rounded. Foliage – alternate, dense, 2-3 inches long. Flower – April and May with new leaves; ½-1 inch wide in clusters of 5 or 6. Fruit – fall; clusters of berrylike apples ½ inch diameter.
Texture	Medium.
Color	Foliage – dark green; fall, yellow-orange. Flower – white. Fruit – dark red.
Culture	Sun. Soil – tolerant in cool areas. Moisture – medium to low. Pruning – remove all understock sprouts. Pest Problems – fire blight and borers. Growth Rate – moderate to slow.
Landscape Notes	Best flowering on mature plants. For large areas as specimen or border.
Variety	*rosea* – red flower buds, flowers pink fading to white.

Spiraea (spy-ree'a)
   Greek for wreath
   or garland

prunifolia (pru-ni-fo'li-a)
   with cherrylike leaves

plena (plee'na)
   double, usually
   doubled flowered

BRIDALWREATH SPIREA

Family Rosaceae

Zones	6, 7, 8.
Size	Height 5-7 feet; spread 3-5 feet.
Form	Upright and graceful with branch tips curving toward ground; medium density. Foliage – alternate, simple, ½-2 inches long, finely toothed. Flower – March; double, like small buttons, in sprays profuse enough to completely cover branches.
Texture	Medium.
Color	Foliage – green; fall, red or orange. Flower – white.
Culture	Sun or shade. Soil – medium drainage; medium fertility. Moisture – medium. Pruning – annual thinning of old canes and spindly growth to ground after flowering. Pest Problems – aphids. Growth Rate – rapid.
Landscape Notes	Valuable shrub for flowers, foliage and fall color; useful for all informal plantings; combines well with perennials and roses.

Spiraea (spy-ree'a)
　　Greek for wreath
　　or garland

vanhouttei (van-hoot'ee-i)
　　named for
　　Louis Van Houtte

VANHOUTTE SPIREA

Family Rosaceae

Zones	6, 7, 8.
Size	Height 5-7 feet; spread 4-6 feet.
Form	Upright semivase with long branches drooping toward ground; medium density. Foliage – alternate, simple, ¾-1¾ inches long. Flower – April; flat clusters ½ inch wide.
Texture	Medium.
Color	Foliage – blue-green. Flower – white.
Culture	Sun or shade. Soil – medium drainage; medium fertility. Moisture – medium. Pruning – annual thinning of old and weak canes to ground after flowering. Pest Problems – aphids. Growth Rate – rapid.
Landscape Notes	Dependable plant which is frequently maintained poorly. Probably most popular of all spireas. Valued for form and flowers; useful as specimen or mass, as natural hedge, or in shrub borders.

Syringa (sir-ring'a)
　　Greek for pipe, referring
　　to hollow stem

persica (per'si-ka)
　　from Persia

PERSIAN LILAC

Family Oleaceae

Zones	6, 7, 8.
Size	Height 6-8 feet; spread 7-9 feet.
Form	Globe-shaped; very dense to medium. Foliage – opposite, simple, heart-shaped, 2 inches long. Flower – mid-April; clusters about 3 inches wide, fragrant.
Texture	Medium.
Color	Foliage – medium green. Flower – lavender pink.
Culture	Sun or part shade. Soil – medium to good drainage; medium fertility; prefers alkaline soil. Moisture – medium. Pruning – annual thinning of old wood and weak sucker growth. Pest Problems – lilac borers, aphids, and mildew. Growth Rate – rapid.
Landscape Notes	Good foliage and twig growth for screening and background. Long lasting plant of high quality with minimum problems. Useful in Southeast where *S. vulgaris* is unsatisfactory.

Syringa (sir-ring'a)
    Greek for pipe, referring
    to hollow stem

vulgaris (vul-gar'is)
    common

COMMON LILAC

Family Oleaceae

Zones	6,7.
Size	Height 10-12 feet; spread 8-10 feet.
Form	Upright shrub or small tree with stiff, ascending spreading branches and irregular outline. Foliage – early spring to late fall; opposite, simple, entire, heart-shaped, 3-4 inches long. Flower – mid-April; panicles about 7 inches long, fragrant. Fruit – summer, persisting through winter; capsule ⅝ inch long.
Texture	Medium to coarse.
Color	Foliage – deep green. Flower – white, pink, and purplish-blue. Fruit – brown.
Culture	Sun. Soil – good drainage; medium fertility; prefers alkaline soil. Moisture – medium. Pruning – remove suckers and faded flowers. Pest Problems – mildew, scale, aphids, and borers. Growth Rate – rapid.
Landscape Notes	Good foliage mass, valued for flowers; useful as specimen or mass and for clipped or unclipped hedges. Many varieties available; buy hybrids on their own roots.
Variety	*alba* – white flowers.

Tamarix (tam'a-ricks)
from Tamaris

gallica (gal'li-ka)
from France

SALTCEDAR

Family Tamaricaceae

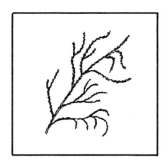

Zones	6, 7, 8.
Size	Height 10-12 feet; spread 9-11 feet.
Form	Broad-spreading, sparse, airy in appearance, sending out slender branches spreading flat and drooping at tips. Foliage – midspring to late fall; tiny, triangular, scalelike. Flower – early spring; dense, terminal racemes 2 inches long. Fruit – fall; inconspicuous.
Texture	Very fine.
Color	Foliage – dull blue-green. Flower – pink.
Culture	Sun. Soil – medium to good drainage; low to medium fertility in sandy loam. Moisture – high. Pruning – very tolerant. Pest Problems – none. Growth Rate – moderate.
Landscape Notes	Salt resistant. Valued for fine and airy texture, pronounced texture accent; useful near sea and mingled in shrub borders; requires facer shrubs. Short lived.
Variety	'Summer Glow' – blooms on new wood in July.

Viburnum (vy-bur'num)
   classical Latin name
   of wayfaring tree

burkwoodii (berk'wood-eye)
   named for A. Burkwood,
   British nurseryman

BURKWOOD VIBURNUM

Family Caprifoliaceae

Zones	6, 7, 8.
Size	Height 6-8 feet; spread 5-7 feet.
Form	Open; irregular to round with age. Foliage – semievergreen in warm areas; opposite, 2-3 inches long; brown veins. Flower – spring with new leaves; ½ inch wide in clusters 3 inches wide, fragrant. Fruit – early fall; clusters of round berries, inconspicuous.
Texture	Medium.
Color	Foliage – lustrous dark green; fall, red. Flower – pinkish-white. Fruit – black.
Culture	Sun or part shade. Soil – good drainage; high to medium fertility. Moisture – high to medium. Pruning – none. Pest Problems – none. Growth Rate – moderate to rapid.
Landscape Notes	For flowering shrub borders, background, and naturalizing in woodlands. May be espaliered on fence or wall. Hybrid of V. *carlesii* and V. *utile*.

Viburnum (vy-bur'num)
　　classical Latin name of
　　wayfaring tree

dilatatum (di-la-ta'tum)
　　dilated, expanded

LINDEN VIBURNUM

Family Caprifoliaceae

Zones	6, 7, 8.
Size	Height 6-9 feet; spread 6-8 feet.
Form	Dense and rounded. Foliage – opposite, 1½ inches wide. Flower – May; profuse flat clusters 5 inches in diameter. Fruit – fall; showy clusters of round berries.
Texture	Medium to coarse.
Color	Foliage – medium green, hairy on both sides; fall, russet-red. Flower – white. Fruit – scarlet-red.
Culture	Sun or part shade. Soil – good drainage; low to medium fertility. Moisture – high to medium. Pruning – none. Pest Problems – none. Growth Rate – moderate.
Landscape Notes	Best flowering and fruiting in open situations and planted in groups. For borders, screens, or specimen use.
Variety	'Xanthocarpum' – yellow fruit.

Viburnum (vy-bur'num)
   classical Latin name
   of wayfaring tree

juddii (judd'i-eye)
   unexplained

JUDD VIBURNUM

Family Caprifoliaceae

Zones	6, 7, 8.
Size	Height 8 feet; spread to 6 feet.
Form	Spreading and rounded, rather dense. Foliage – opposite, 2 inches wide, toothed, deeply veined. Flower – early spring; loose clusters 3½ inches wide, slightly fragrant. Fruit – fall; berrylike.
Texture	Coarse.
Color	Foliage – deep green, downy beneath. Flower – white. Fruit – reddish-black.
Culture	Sun or part shade. Soil – good drainage; medium to high fertility. Moisture – high. Pruning – remove winterkilled parts. Pest Problems – none. Growth Rate – rapid.
Landscape Notes	Useful as background or in mixed shrub borders. Fragrance of flowers pleasing. Excellent specimen or accent. Fruit attracts birds. Hybrid between *V. carlesii* and *V. bitchuense*.

Viburnum (vy-bur'num)
    classical Latin name
    of wayfaring tree

plicatum (ply-kay'tum)
    plaited or folded in plaits

tomentosum (toe-men-toe'sum)
    densely covered with matted,
    flat hairs

DOUBLEFILE VIBURNUM

Family Caprifoliaceae

Zones	6, 7, 8.
Size	Height 8-10 feet; spread 8-10 feet.
Form	Strong and vigorous with broad-spreading, almost horizontal branches. Foliage – midspring to midfall; opposite, 3-4 inches long with marked veins. Flower – April, after leaves; 4 inches wide, flat-topped cymes held above branches with sterile flowers bordering cluster. Fruit – summer; small drupes.
Texture	Coarse.
Color	Foliage – deep green; fall, deep red. Flower – white. Fruit – red turning black.
Culture	Sun or part shade. Soil – tolerant; medium drainage; medium fertility. Moisture – medium to high. Pruning – when needed to renew growth. Pest Problems – none. Growth Rate – moderate.
Landscape Notes	Very handsome specimen or accent plant; useful in shrub borders. Beautiful horizontal branching habit displaying flowers and fruit well. Will not tolerate drought.

Vitex (vy'tex)
   ancient Latin name

agnus-castus (ag'nus-cast'us)
   ancient classical name for
   chaste lamb

CHASTE-TREE

Family Verbenaceae

Zones	6, 7, 8.
Size	Height 10-12 feet; spread 8-10 feet.
Form	Semiglobe, open and irregular if not cut back each year. Foliage – late spring; opposite, 5-parted, with leaflets 1-4 inches long. Flower – July; small spikes. Fruit – fall; ¼ inch thick dry berries, aromatic. Twigs – 4 angled.
Texture	Medium.
Color	Foliage – gray-green. Flower – pale violet. Fruit – blue-black.
Culture	Sun or part shade. Soil – very tolerant; medium to good drainage; medium fertility. Moisture – medium to low. Pruning – cut back to ground every year or every few years for compactness and general appearance. Pest Problems – none. Growth Rate – rapid.
Landscape Notes	Foliage has pungent, aromatic, sagelike odor. Handsome mass, particularly attractive in bloom, but difficult to blend with other shrubs. May be used as small tree if unpruned.
Varieties	'Alba' – white flowers. 'Rosea' – pink flowers.

Weigela (wy-gee'la)
  named for C.E. Weigel

florida (flo'ri-da)
  freely flowering

WEIGELA

Family Caprifoliaceae

Zones	6, 7, 8.
Size	Height 6-8 feet; spread 8-10 feet.
Form	Erect and spreading branches finally arching to ground. Foliage – midspring to midfall; opposite, 4 inches long. Flower – late April or early May; very showy, bell-shaped, profuse clusters of 3 to 5. Fruit – late summer; smooth capsules splitting in 2 halves.
Texture	Coarse.
Color	Foliage – medium green to deep green; fall, slightly yellow. Flower – pink. Fruit – tan-brown.
Culture	Sun. Soil – tolerant; medium drainage; medium fertility. Moisture – high. Pruning – remove old branches and winter-killed twigs. Pest Problems – none. Growth Rate – moderate.
Landscape Notes	Valued for handsome flowers; at other seasons rather coarse, does not blend well with other shrubs; best as specimen or accent in very large gardens.
Varieties	*alba* – white flowers. 'Variegata' – leaves bordered with yellow; deep rose flowers.

SMALL TREES — EVERGREEN

Eriobotrya (ear-i-o-bot′ri-a)
  Greek for woolly cluster,
  in allusion to hairy
  flower cluster

japonica (ja-pon′i-ka)
  from Japan

LOQUAT

Family Rosaceae

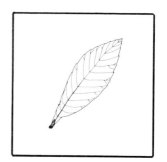

Zones	7, 8.
Size	Height 10-20 feet; spread 8-12 feet.
Form	Dense rounded head on short slender trunk. Foliage – alternate, 5-10 inches long, glossy above, tomentose beneath. Flower – November; ½ inch diameter, fragrant. Fruit – ripening in April; 1½ inches long, pear-shaped, edible.
Texture	Coarse.
Color	Foliage – dark green above, rusty beneath. Flower – white. Fruit – yellow.
Culture	Sun or part shade. Soil – good drainage; medium fertility. Moisture – medium. Pruning – none. Pest Problems – usually none but can develop pear blight. Growth Rate – rapid.
Landscape Notes	Excellent specimen or accent plant, especially effective against architectural background. May be used in shrub borders, planter boxes, or as screen. Adaptable to any size area. Interesting espaliered.

Ilex (eye'lecks)
   hollies

cassine (ka-seen')
   from Timucua Indians

DAHOON

Family Aquifoliaceae

Zones	7,8.
Size	Height 20-30 feet; spread 10-15 feet.
Form	Large shrub or small tree, usually single trunked; rounded with dense branching. Foliage – alternate, 1½-4 inches long, entire or with slight serrations. Flower – inconspicuous. Fruit – fall and winter; ¼ inch berries in clusters.
Texture	Fine.
Color	Foliage – green to yellow-green; fall, purple-green. Fruit – red.
Culture	Sun or part shade. Soil – tolerant; prefers sandy loam. Moisture – medium to high. Pruning – none. Pest Problems – none. Growth Rate – medium.
Landscape Notes	Remains somewhat shrubby in colder areas. Native to swampy locations, good for naturalizing in these areas. Interesting grey bark, evergreen foliage, and attractive fruit.
Variety	'Angustifolia' – Alabama Dahoon; narrow, linear leaves; much improved selection.

Ilex (eye'lecks)
  hollies

myrtifolia (mert-i-fo'li-a)
  leaves like myrtle

MYRTLE-LEAVED HOLLY

Family Aquifoliaceae

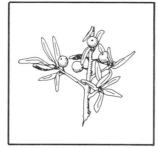

Zone	8.
Size	Height 20 feet; spread 7-9 feet.
Form	Narrow and rounded with open branches. Foliage – alternate, entire, 1-2 inches long, oblong to linear. Flower spring, on current season's wood; inconspicuous. Fruit – fall and winter; berrylike drupe, ¼ inch diameter.
Texture	Fine.
Color	Foliage – dark green above, pale beneath. Flower – white. Fruit – red, rarely yellow.
Culture	Part shade. Soil – good drainage; medium to high fertility. Moisture – high. Pruning – none. Pest Problems – leaf miner. Growth Rate – moderate.
Landscape Notes	Grown for attractive habit, foliage, and berries. Excellent for tall screens or borders.
Variety	'Lowii' – yellow berries and dark green foliage.

Ilex (eye'lecks)
  hollies

opaca (o-pay'ka)
  opaque or pale

AMERICAN HOLLY

Family Aquifoliaceae

Zones	6, 7, 8.
Size	Height 15-30 feet; spread 10-20 feet.
Form	Upright and conical with horizontal branches or open in poor growing conditions; medium density. Foliage – alternate, 2-4 inches long, 1-2 inches wide, stiff and leathery, not lustrous, margins usually spiny-toothed. Flower – spring; inconspicuous, male and female flowers on separate plants. Fruit – fall and winter; berrylike, ¼ inch diameter; both male and female plants must be present for fruit.
Texture	Medium to slightly coarse.
Color	Foliage – dark green, light green beneath. Flower – white. Fruit – red. Bark – gray, smooth.
Culture	Sun to part shade. Soil – good drainage; medium fertility. Moisture – medium to high. Pruning – balance and retain central leader. Pest Problems – leaf miner. Growth Rate – slow.
Landscape Notes	Foliage sometimes disfigured by winter sun. Difficult to transplant from wild. Best employed as specimen plant or in clumps as screen and border material. Fruit production best in full sun. Allow lower limbs to branch to ground naturally. Interesting topiary. Will not tolerate direct salt spray.
Variety	'East Palatka' – small, light green leaves; adapted to moist, protected situations; dark red fruit.

Pinus (py'nus)
old Latin
name for pine

nigra (ny'gra)
black

AUSTRIAN PINE

Family Pinaceae

Zones	6, 7, 8.
Size	Height 20-40 feet; spread 12-20 feet.
Form	Conical, semiround top; medium density. Foliage – 2 needles per bundle, 3-6 inches long. Fruit – cones 2-4 inches long.
Texture	Medium.
Color	Foliage – medium green. Fruit – greenish-brown.
Culture	Sun. Soil – good drainage; medium fertility. Moisture – medium. Pruning – maintain central leader and general balance. Pest Problems – pine-tip moth and pine needle blight. Growth Rate – moderate.
Landscape Notes	Picturesque with age. Easily transplanted. Use as texture contrast in shrub borders or as screen when spaced 12-15 feet apart. Fairly tolerant of seashore conditions.

Prunus (proo'nus)
   classical Latin
   name of plum

caroliniana (ka-ro-lin-i-a'na)
   from Carolinas

CAROLINA CHERRY-LAUREL

Family Rosaceae

Zones	7, 8.
Size	Height 20-30 feet; spread 15-20 feet.
Form	Dense rounded head with single trunk or rounded and shrubby. Foliage – alternate, 2-4 inches long. Flower – March to April; short racemes 2-5 inches long, fragrant. Fruit – fall; ½ inch long.
Texture	Medium.
Color	Foliage – glossy dark green. Flower – white. Fruit – black.
Culture	Sun or part shade. Soil – well-drained; medium fertility. Moisture – medium. Pruning – tolerant. Pest Problems – none. Growth Rate – rapid.
Landscape Notes	Excellent in natural form; may be sheared for hedges or topiary work. Grown primarily for excellent foliage. Forms good wind break. Use as specimen, screen, or border. Difficult to transplant in large sizes. Not cold hardy in mountain areas.
Variety	'Compacta' – dense, compact habit of growth.

Quercus (kwer'kus)
  clasical Latin
  name for oak

acuta (a-cu'ta)
  with acute leaves

JAPANESE EVERGREEN OAK

Family Fagaceae

Zones	7, 8.
Size	Height 20-40 feet; spread 8-16 feet.
Form	Rounded with low branching to ground; multiple trunks. Foliage – alternate, 3-5 inches long, toothed at upper end. Flower – inconspicuous. Fruit – small acorn.
Texture	Coarse.
Color	Foliage – glossy olive-green with grayish cast on underside. Bark – smooth, gray.
Culture	Sun. Soil – good drainage; medium to high fertility. Moisture – medium. Pruning – shape. Pest Problems – none. Growth Rate – moderate.
Landscape Notes	Specimen or screening material with heavy low branching and elegant foliage.

Sabal (say'bal)
   unexplained

palmetto (pal-met'to)
   little palm

PALMETTO

Family Palmaceae

Zone	8.
Size	Height 20-30 feet; spread 10-15 feet.
Form	Straight, single trunk with compact crown, upper portion of trunk covered with persistant leaf bases. Foliage – to 5-6 feet long and 4-7 feet across, deeply cut, palmate. Flower – spring; ⅓ inch diameter in drooping clusters 2-2½ feet long, fragrant. Fruit – fall; ⅓ inch diameter.
Texture	Medium.
Color	Foliage – lustrous green. Flower – white. Fruit – black.
Culture	Sun or shade. Soil – very tolerant; medium drainage; medium fertility. Moisture – high. Pruning – none. Pest Problems – palmetto weevil and palm leaf skeletonizer. Growth Rate – moderate.
Landscape Notes	Excellent as street tree, specimen, patio, or terrace tree. Creates interesting shadow patterns against walls. Very tolerant of salt, recommended for seaside plantings. Easy to transplant in June and July. Not hardy in Piedmont or mountain areas.

Trachycarpus (trayk-i-karp'us)
 from Greek for rough or
 harsh and for fruit

fortunei (for-too'nee-i)
 named for Robert Fortune

WINDMILL PALM

Family Palmaceae

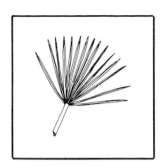

Zone	8.
Size	Height 15-35 feet; spread 10-15 feet.
Form	Trunk solitary and post-like; covered with black hair-like fiber. Foliage – fan-shaped, 2-3 feet wide. Flower – spring; small, in large panicles to 2 feet long.
Texture	Coarse.
Color	Foliage – medium to dull green. Flower – yellow.
Culture	Part shade with wind protection. Soil – good drainage; medium fertility with organic matter added. Moisture – high when young. Pruning – remove dead leaves. Pest Problems – scale. Growth Rate – rapid.
Landscape Notes	Cold tender but will not tolerate extreme heat. Frequently used in containers and as street tree. Transplant in spring or summer when roots are active. Excellent trunk effect; strong accent plant.

SMALL TREES — DECIDUOUS

Acer (a'sir)
 ancient Latin name
 of maple

palmatum (pal-may'tum)
 with leaflets or with
 lobes or veins of leaf
 radiating from one point

JAPANESE MAPLE

Family Aceraceae

Zones	6,7,8.
Size	Height 15-20 feet; spread 10-15 feet.
Form	Low and round-topped with open, irregular crown, and ascending, spreading branches. Foliage – opposite, simple, palmately lobed, 2-4 inches across. Flower – March; erect clusters. Fruit – spring; samara, 1 inch long, 2 winged.
Texture	Medium.
Color	Foliage – green to red; fall, scarlet. Flower – purple-red. Fruit – red.
Culture	Part shade. Soil – good drainage; high fertility. Moisture – medium. Pruning – shape. Pest Problems – maple insects and diseases. Growth Rate – slow.
Landscape Notes	Beautiful tree for small gardens and terraces. Refined in character. Many varieties useful as specimens or accent plants in borders and rock gardens. Difficult to transplant.
Varieties	'Atropurpureum' – dark red leaves; small 5-lobed leaf. *dissectum* – unequalled in grace and beauty; delicately cut red leaves. Excellent specimen. Height 4-6 feet.

Albizia (al-bizz'ee-a)
named for Albizzi,
Italian naturalist

julibrissin (jew-lee-bris'in)
Persian vernacular
for silk tree

MIMOSA

Family Fabaceae

Zones	6, 7, 8.
Size	Height 20-30 feet; spread 25-30 feet.
Form	Spreading, low, and fairly open. Foliage – alternate, twice compound, 12-18 inches long. Flower – June and July; silky pompoms 2 inches in diameter, fragrant. Fruit – late summer and fall; flattened pods 4-6 inches long.
Texture	Fine.
Color	Foliage – gray-green. Flower – rose-red to pink. Fruit – brown. Bark – light gray.
Culture	Sun. Soil – medium to good drainage; medium fertility. Moisture – medium. Pruning – train young trees to prevent weak branch formation. Pest Problems – mimosa wilt disease and webworms. Growth Rate – rapid.
Landscape Notes	Comparatively short life, breaks easily. Low branching habit creates circulation problems for some locations. Interesting small temporary shade tree or specimen. Germinates freely from seed. Difficult to transplant large sizes.
Varieties	'Charlotte' — wilt-resistant. 'Ernest Wilson' — flower bright pink; hardier than species. 'Tryon' — wilt-resistant.

Amelanchier (am-e-lank'i-er)
unexplained

canadensis (kan-a-den'sis)
from Canada

SERVICEBERRY

Family Rosaceae

Zones	6, 7, 8.
Size	Height 10-20 feet; spread 8-15 feet.
Form	Upright, irregular, and graceful; medium density. May be multi-trunked. Foliage – alternate, simple, toothed, base usually rounded, 2-3 inches long. Flower – spring; racemes 2 inches long. Fruit – June; berrylike, edible.
Texture	Medium.
Color	Foliage – medium green, gray in early spring; fall, red to yellow. Flower – white. Fruit – dark red. Bark – light gray.
Culture	Sun or part shade. Soil – very tolerant; medium drainage; medium fertility. Moisture – medium. Pruning – thin side branches for shape. Pest Problems – leaf defoliators, scale, borer, and fire blight. Growth Rate – moderate.
Landscape Notes	Blooms just before dogwood. Attractive with background of loblolly pines or planted along edge of wild areas. Native to mountains of Southeast.

Betula (bet'you-la)
   classical name
   of birch

nigra (ny'gra)
   black

RIVER BIRCH

Family Betulaceae

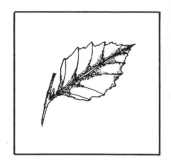

Zones	6, 7, 8.
Size	Height 20-40 feet; spread 16-20 feet.
Form	Upright and open with thin and slightly drooping twigs. Foliage – alternate, simple, double toothed, 1½-3 inches long. Flower – inconspicuous hanging catkins. Fruit – late spring; samara ¼ inch long. Bark – exfoliating, papery.
Texture	Fine to medium.
Color	Foliage – medium green, whitish beneath; fall, rich yellow. Fruit – brown. Bark – reddish-brown.
Culture	Part shade. Soil – medium drainage; medium to high fertility. Moisture – high. Pruning – not tolerant. Pest Problems – none. Growth Rate – moderate.
Landscape Notes	Frequently seen along creeks and streams in southeast. Grows well on high or low ground. Adaptable to multiple trunk. Graceful branching habit; interesting informal tree for lawns or gardens. Select specimens with thin trunks and low arching branches for best effect.

Betula (bet'you-la)
 classical name
 of birch

pendula (pen'dew-la)
 pendulous, hanging

EUROPEAN WHITE BIRCH

Family Betulaceae

Zones	6, 7.
Size	Height 20-40 feet; spread 8-16 feet.
Form	Slender, rounded, and graceful; pendulous in age with fine and hazy winter effect. Foliage – alternate, simple, double toothed, 1½-3 inches long. Flower – early spring; catkins. Fruit – small samara. Bark – peeling.
Texture	Fine.
Color	Foliage – light green. Flower – pale yellow. Bark – chalky white to creamy white.
Culture	Sun. Soil – medium drainage; medium fertility. Moisture – high. Pruning – not very tolerant; remove dead wood and broken branches. Pest Problems – bronze birch borer; sometimes host of fungus disease of Larch. Growth Rate – fairly rapid.
Landscape Notes	Difficult to transplant and short lived. Unrivaled in lightness, grace and elegance; light accent, useful as specimen. Multiple trunk forms usually available. Good in mountains and upper southeast.
Varieties	'Fastigiata' – dense and columnar. 'Gracilis' – finely dissected leaves; pendulous branches.

Carpinus (kar-py'nus)
ancient name
of hornbeam

caroliniana (ka-ro-lin-i-a'na)
from Carolinas

AMERICAN HORNBEAM

Family Betulaceae

Zones	6, 7, 8.
Size	Height 20-30 feet; spread 15-20 feet.
Form	Refined in character; light and informal growth with horizontal branching. Foliage – alternate, simple, double toothed, 2-4 inches long, parallel venation. Flower – spring; hanging catkins. Fruit – summer; small winged nut. Bark – smoothly ridged or knotted.
Texture	Fine.
Color	Foliage – dull green; fall, reddish. Flower – green. Fruit – black. Bark – gray.
Culture	Sun or shade. Soil – tolerant; medium drainage; medium fertility. Moisture – medium. Pruning – tolerant. Pest Problems – none. Growth Rate – very slow.
Landscape Notes	Good street or shade tree with refined character; also for hedges, game-cover, and natural areas. Trunk interesting for sculptural appearance. Transplant while young.

Cercis (sir'sis)
  ancient Greek name

canadensis (kan-a-den'sis)
  from Canada

EASTERN REDBUD

Family Fabaceae

Zones	6, 7, 8.
Size	Height 20-30 feet; spread 12-25 feet.
Form	Dense and round in sun, loose and open in shade. Foliage – alternate, heart-shaped to 5 inches long, 3-5 inches wide. Flower – March and April before leaves appear; small and pealike, in clusters nearly covering bare branches. Fruit – late summer and fall; long, flattened pods.
Texture	Medium to coarse.
Color	Foliage – dark green; fall, yellow. Flower – lavender-pink. Fruit – green turning brown.
Culture	Sun or part shade. Soil – good drainage; medium fertility. Moisture – medium. Pruning – encourage low branching; multiple trunk desirable. Pest Problems – leaf rollers, aphids, spider mites, and leaf diseases. Growth Rate – slow to moderate.
Landscape Notes	Good foliage and very beautiful in blossom; interesting specimen or filler. Very drought resistant. Fruit sometimes unsightly when mature. Difficult to transplant when large or from woodlands.
Varieties	'Alba' – white flowers. Outstanding specimen tree. 'Withers Pink Charm' – flowers soft pale pink.

Cornus (kor'nus)
   Latin horn, from
   toughness of wood

florida (flo'ri-da)
   freely flowering

FLOWERING DOGWOOD

Family Cornaceae

Zones	6, 7, 8.
Size	Height 15-30 feet; spread 15-20 feet.
Form	Semiround top with horizontal branching; dense to fairly open; single or multitrunked. Foliage – opposite, simple, entire or somewhat wavy, 3-6 inches long. Flower – mid-April; small compact heads surrounded by 4 petallike bracts. Fruit – fall; ovoid, in clusters. Bark – scalelike.
Texture	Medium.
Color	Foliage – medium green; fall, scarlet. Flower – white. Fruit – red.
Culture	Part shade. Soil – good drainage; medium fertility. Moisture – medium. Pruning – remove half of top if transplanting bare-root. Pest Problems – dogwood borers under bark and anthracnose on foliage. Growth Rate – moderate.
Landscape Notes	Interesting horizontal branch structure. Use in group plantings or as accent in borders and margins of woods and undergrowth. Most popular of flowering trees with year-round interest. Develops thinner and more graceful habit in part shade rather than full sun.
Varieties	*plena* – double flowers. 'White Cloud' – profusion of creamy-white flowers. 'Xanthocarpa' – yellow fruit.

Cornus (kor'nus)
Latin horn, from
toughness of wood

kousa (kou'suh)
Japanese vernacular
name

KOUSA DOGWOOD

Family Cornaceae

Zones	6, 7.
Size	Height 10-15 feet; spread 10 feet.
Form	Large shrub or small tree; single or multistem with horizontal branching. Foliage – opposite, dense, 4 inches long. Flower – early May; inconspicuous, surrounded by large pointed bracts 1½-2 inches long. Fruit – late summer; raspberrylike, ½-1 inch diameter.
Texture	Medium.
Color	Foliage – lustrous green; fall, scarlet. Flower – white. Fruit – pinkish-red.
Culture	Sun or part shade. Soil – good drainage; medium fertility. Moisture – medium. Pruning – shape. Pest Problems – borers. Growth Rate – moderate.
Landscape Notes	Blooms after leaves appear. Useful as specimen or accent in background; excellent border or hedge for large areas. Attractive against large evergreens.
Varieties	*chinensis* – Chinese Dogwood. Bracts slightly longer (2-3½ inches) than species; scarlet autumn leaf coloring. 'Milky Way' – profusely flowering selection of *C. kousa chinensis*.

Cotinus (ko-ty'nus)
ancient Greek name
for tree with red wood

coggyria (kog-jeeg'ree-uh)
ancient Greek name

SMOKETREE

Family Anacardiaceae

Zones	6, 7, 8.
Size	Height 10-15 feet; spread 8-14 feet.
Form	Shrub or small tree; open and irregular. Foliage – alternate, 3 inches long, oval. Flower – June and July; inconspicuous clusters. Fruit – August and September; 7-10 inch panicles on female plants; stalks of fruiting panicles create smoky effect.
Texture	Medium.
Color	Foliage – reddish turning green; fall, red, orange, or yellow. Flower – greenish-yellow. Fruit – light pink to gray.
Culture	Sun. Soil – good drainage; low fertility. Moisture – low when established. Pruning – remove dead branches. Pest Problems – nematodes and verticillium wilt. Growth Rate – moderate to rapid in sandy soils.
Landscape Notes	Maintain high moisture until well established. Interesting specimen or border plant for cooler areas.
Varieties	'Daydream' – large purple-pink fruiting panicles. 'Purpureus' – purplish leaves and purple-pink fruiting panicles.

Elaeagnus (eel-ee-ag'nus)
  from Greek for olive
  and chaste tree

angustifolius (an-gus-teę-fo'li-us)
  narrow-leaved

RUSSIAN-OLIVE

Family Elaeagnaceae

Zones	6, 7, 8.
Size	Height 15-20 feet; spread 20-30 feet.
Form	Wide-spreading and open. Foliage – late spring to late fall; alternate, simple, entire, 2-3½ inches long. Flower – late spring; inconspicuous, fragrant. Fruit – summer to late fall; ½ inch long, egg-shaped.
Texture	Fine.
Color	Foliage – silver-gray. Flower – yellow. Fruit – yellow with silvery scales.
Culture	Sun. Soil – tolerant; medium drainage; medium fertility. Moisture – low to medium. Pruning – maintain desired shape and remove dead twigs. Pest Problems – none. Growth Rate – rapid.
Landscape Notes	Withstands severe exposures. Of value for rapid growth. Use as accent, hedge, or light-toned mass against evergreen background. Rather short lived.

Franklinia (frank-lin'i-a)
   named for Benjamin Franklin

alatamaha (al-tah-ma'ha)
   named for Alatamaha River,
   Georgia

FRANKLINIA

Family Theaceae

Zones	6, 7, 8.
Size	Height 20-30 feet; spread 15-18 feet.
Form	Pyramidal with spreading branches; large shrub or small tree. Foliage – midspring to midfall; alternate, simple, finely toothed, 5-7 inches long, lustrous above, pubescent beneath. Flower – September to October; 3 inch diameter, clustered buds developing singly, each lasting several days, cup-shaped, fragrant.
Texture	Coarse.
Color	Foliage – glossy green; fall, brilliant red or orange. Flower – white with yellow stamens.
Culture	Sun. Soil – medium drainage; high fertility. Moisture – medium to high. Pruning – shape and clean. Pest Problems – none. Growth Rate – moderate to slow.
Landscape Notes	Valued for showy, fragrant late summer flowers and colorful autumn foliage. Use as accent, specimen, or filler in shrub borders. Difficult to transplant successfully.

Halesia (hal-ee'si-a)
silverbell

monticola (mon-tik'o-la)
inhabiting mountains

MOUNTAIN SILVERBELL

Family Styracaceae

Zones	6, 7.
Size	Height 20-40 feet; spread 20 feet.
Form	Rounded, open, irregular. Foliage – alternate, 3-7 inches long. Flower – mid-April; bell-shaped, pendulous, 1 inch long, 2-5 in cluster. Fruit – fall; dry winged pods 2 inches long. Bark – scales large and loose.
Texture	Medium to coarse.
Color	Foliage – light green; fall, yellow. Flower – white. Fruit – translucent yellow, turning brown.
Culture	Part shade or shade. Soil – good drainage; medium to low fertility. Moisture – medium. Pruning – none. Pest Problems – none. Growth Rate – slow to moderate.
Landscape Notes	Attractive multistem small tree. Interesting effect with night lighting against evergreen background. Useful in borders and along paths or streets where flowers can be seen. Excellent as naturalizing material.
Variety	*rosea* – pale pink flowers.

Hamamelis (ham-am-ee'lis)
Greek for together and apple;
flowers and fruit
appear together

mollis (mol'lis)
soft

CHINESE WITCH-HAZEL

Family Hamamelidaceae

Zones	6, 7.
Size	Height 15-20 feet; spread 8-10 feet.
Form	Graceful and broadly spreading. Young twigs and buds pubescent. Foliage – alternate, 4-7 inches long. Flower – February to March; 1½ inches wide with 4 ribbonlike petals, very fragrant. Fruit – dry capsule.
Texture	Coarse.
Color	Foliage – medium green; fall, bright yellow. Flower – bright yellow. Fruit – brown with black seeds.
Culture	Sun or part shade. Soil – medium drainage; medium fertility with humus added. Moisture – medium to high. Pruning – train to tree form if desired. Pest Problems – none. Growth Rate – slow to moderate.
Landscape Notes	Valued for very early spring flowering and beautiful autumn coloring. For specimen use or naturalizing.
Variety	'Pallida' – conspicuous lemon-yellow flowers.

Koelreuteria (kel-roo-teer'i-a)
  named for
  Joseph G. Koelreuter

paniculata (pan-ick-kew-lay'ta)
  compound raceme

GOLDEN-RAIN-TREE

Family Sapindaceae

Zones	6, 7, 8.
Size	Height 20-30 feet; spread 15-20 feet.
Form	Upright, irregular; medium to open density. Foliage – alternate, single or double pinnately compound, 9-14 inches long. Flower – June; pyramidal clusters 1-1½ feet long. Fruit – midsummer to fall; clusters of 2 inch papery pods.
Texture	Medium.
Color	Foliage – dark green. Flower – yellow. Fruit – light brown.
Culture	Sun or part shade. Soil – good drainage essential; medium fertility. Moisture – medium. Pruning – remove weak limbs. Pest Problems – none. Growth Rate – moderate to rapid.
Landscape Notes	Foliage similar to chinaberry. Valuable for flower and showy seed pods. Best used in groups; withstands city conditions. Short lived.

Laburnum (la-bur'num)
  ancient Latin name

anagyroides (a-na-ju-roy'deez)
  bearing recurved pods

GOLDEN-CHAIN

Family Fabaceae

Zones	6, 7.
Size	Height 20-30 feet; spread 10-15 feet.
Form	Stiff and upright; multitrunked; sparsely branched with erect or ascending branches. Foliage – alternate, compound with leaflets 1½-2½ inches long, cloverlike and silky pubescent when young. Flower – May after leaves appear; pendulous clusters to 12 inches long, pealike, profuse. Fruit – mid-summer, long persistent; pods 12 inches long; seeds very poisonous.
Texture	Fine.
Color	Foliage – bright green. Flower – bright yellow. Fruit – green turning black.
Culture	Sun. Soil – well-drained; medium fertility. Moisture – medium. Pruning – shape. Pest Problems – mildew. Growth Rate – slow.
Landscape Notes	Exotic; occasionally useful as specimen or in masses. Adapted for planting on rocky slopes. Foliage often harmed by frost; rather short-lived. Needs protection from winds and drought.

Lagerstroemia (lay-ger-stree'mi-a)
named for Magnus
von Lagerstroem

indica (in'di-ka)
from India

CRAPE-MYRTLE

Family Lythraceae

Zones	6,7,8.
Size	Height 15-25 feet; spread 5-15 feet.
Form	Upright and open or rounded; multiple trunk with dense branching. Foliage – emerging in late spring; opposite, 1-2 inches long. Flower – July and August; dense clusters 1 0 inches long on new wood.
Texture	Medium.
Color	Foliage – medium green; fall, yellow, red, or rust-red. Flower – white, pink, red, or lavender. Bark – pale gray-brown, shredding to reveal lighter underbark.
Culture	Sun. Soil – medium to good drainage; medium to high fertility. Moisture – medium to high. Pruning – lightly for shape. Pest Problems – mildew when grown in shade. Growth Rate – moderate.
Landscape Notes	Decorative and effective throughout year as specimen or multi-trunked small tree. Not screening material; use with evergreen background. May be pruned annually to ground to maintain shrub size. Difficult to transplant large sizes.

Magnolia (mag-no'li-a)
named for Pierre Magnol

soulangiana (su-lan'gee-ana)
named for C.Soulange-Bodin

SAUCER MAGNOLIA

Family Magnoliaceae

Zones	6, 7, 8.
Size	Height 15-25 feet; spread 15-25 feet.
Form	Upright and irregular with open branching. Foliage – alternate, simple, entire, 4-6 inches long. Flower – March before leaves appear; cup-shaped, 6 inch diameter.
Texture	Medium to coarse.
Color	Foliage – medium green. Flower – purple to white. Bark – gray-brown.
Culture	Sun or part shade. Soil – medium to good drainage; medium to high fertility. Moisture – medium to high. Pruning – none. Pest Problems – scale. Growth Rate – moderate.
Landscape Notes	Best suited to city gardens; espaliers well in limited areas. Often begins blooming when very young. Select late-blooming varieties to avoid damage from late freezes.
Varieties	'Alba' – compact growth habit; white flowers. 'Brozzoni' – white flowers, 10 inch diameter. 'Speciosa' – pale pink-white flowers; late-blooming. 'Verbanica' – flowers rose pink and white; late blooming.

Malus (may'lus)
    ancient Latin name
    of apple

hybrida (hy'brid-a)
    hybrid

FLOWERING CRAB APPLE

Family Rosaceae

Zones	6, 7, 8.
Size	Height 15-25 feet; spread 10-20 feet.
Form	Round to spreading crown with irregular or horizontal branching. Foliage – alternate, 1-3 inches long. Flower – April; 1-2 inches wide in clusters. Fruit – midsummer; ¼-1½ inch diameter.
Texture	Medium.
Color	Foliage – medium green. Flower – white to rose. Fruit – red or yellow.
Culture	Sun. Soil – medium drainage; medium fertility. Moisture – medium. Pruning – develop central trunk. Pest Problems – leaf defoliators, scale, fire blight, and rust. Growth Rate – moderate.
Landscape Notes	More susceptible to fire blight when forced by too much fertilizing or heavy pruning. Many fine species available for specimen use and massing, such as *M. floribunda, M. arnoldiana, M. sargentii,* and *M. toringoides.*
Varieties	'Dorothea' – semidouble rose flowers; yellow fruit. 'Hopa' – rose flowers; new foliage maroon tinted.

Malus (may'lus)
  ancient Latin name
  of apple

pumila (pew'mi-la)
  dwarf

APPLE

Family Rosaceae

Zones	6, 7, 8.
Size	Height 25-40 feet; spread 25-40 feet.
Form	Spreading to semiround top, compact. Foliage – alternate, 2-4 inches long. Flower – spring; clusters borne on spurs. Fruit – late summer; pome.
Texture	Medium.
Color	Foliage – dark green. Flower – pinkish-white. Fruit – yellow to red.
Culture	Sun. Soil – medium to good drainage; medium fertility. Moisture – medium. Pruning – train for strength of branches. Pest Problems – scale, fruit worms, cedar apple rust, scab, blotch, and fire blight. Growth Rate – moderate.
Landscape Notes	Develops rugged, sculptural form with careful pruning. Size between 8-15 feet controlled by use of dwarfing rootstocks; cross-pollination required for good fruiting in some varieties. Follow regular spray schedule.
Varieties	'Golden Delicious' – yellow apples; self-fruitful. 'Red Delicious' – cross-pollination necessary. 'Red Rome' – very late ripening; self-fruitful.

Oxydendrum (ok-si-den'drum)
Greek for sour tree, from
acid taste of foliage

arboreum (ar-bore'ee-um)
treelike

SOURWOOD

Family Ericaceae

Zones	6, 7, 8.
Size	Height 20-30 feet; spread 10-15 feet.
Form	Erect with slender trunk and slender upright branches, oval to cylindrical crown. Foliage – alternate, simple, toothed, to 8 inches long. Flower – summer; terminal clusters of one-sided racemes, spreading and curving out and up. Fruit – late fall, persisting; ovoid-pyramidal capsules.
Texture	Coarse.
Color	Foliage – shiny green; fall, brillant red. Flower – white. Fruit – gray. Bark – reddish-gray, branchlets brown or reddish.
Culture	Sun or shade. Soil – medium drainage; medium fertility; prefers acid soil. Moisture – medium to low. Pruning – trim for shape. Pest Problems – fall webworm. Growth Rate – slow.
Landscape Notes	Slender and handsome; valued for summer flowering and for brilliant fall coloring; useful in borders and as undercover in woodland. Best effect when planted in groups. Easy to transplant when young.

Prunus (proo'nus)
   classical Latin name
   of plum

cerasifera (ser-ra-sif'fer-ra)
   bearing cherries or
   cherrylike fruit

'Atropurpurea' (at-ro-per-pu're-a)
   dark purple

PISSARD PLUM

Family Rosaceae

Zones	6, 7, 8.
Size	Height 15-20 feet; spread 10-15 feet.
Form	Smaller than domestic plum, twiggy and rounded, with ascending, spreading branches. Foliage – early spring to midfall; alternate, simple, 1½-2 inches long. Flower – spring with leaves; ¾ inch wide, often crowded on short twigs. Fruit – early summer; subglobose, 1 inch diameter, edible.
Texture	Medium.
Color	Foliage – reddish-purple. Flower – pinkish-white. Fruit – purple. Bark – dark gray.
Culture	Sun. Soil – medium drainage; medium fertility. Moisture – medium. Pruning – remove crossed branches. Pest Problems – fruit insects and diseases. Growth Rate – moderate to rapid.
Landscape Notes	Use as specimen or accent. Withstands hot, dry conditions. Ornamental varieties with colored foliage suitable for limited landscape use.

Prunus (proo'nus)
classical Latin name
of plum

cerasus (ser'a-sus)
name for cherry

SOUR CHERRY

Family Rosaceae

Zones	6,7,8.
Size	Height 20-30 feet; spread 15-20 feet.
Form	Rounded with open branching, light in effect. Foliage – alternate, simple, serrated, glabrous, 2-3½ inches long with petioles to 1 inch long. Flower – April, before leaves appear; single, ¾-1 inch wide in small clusters; self-fertile. Fruit – early summer; drupe ¾ inch diameter in small clusters, edible.
Texture	Medium.
Color	Foliage – light green. Flower – white. Fruit – shiny red to black. Bark – shiny black.
Culture	Sun or part shade. Soil – medium drainage; medium fertility. Moisture – medium. Pruning – remove weak and crossed branches. Pest Problems – usually none; occasionally caterpillars and virus diseases. Growth Rate – moderate.
Landscape Notes	Excellent form and pleasing natural appearance all seasons; flowers most effective against evergreen background. Tolerant of shaded situations in light woodlands or may be used as specimen or espaliered. Fruit attracts birds; avoid placing near drives, walks, and patios. Easily transplanted while young; lives 15-20 years.

Prunus (proo'nus)
   classical Latin
   name of plum

persica (per'si-ka)
   from Persia

PEACH

Family Rosaceae

Zones	6, 7, 8.
Size	Height 10-15 feet; spread 10-15 feet.
Form	Rounded or low and spreading when center opened by pruning. Medium density. Foliage – alternate, simple, toothed, slightly folded along midrib, 3-6 inches long. Flower – early spring before leaves appear; single or double, 1-1½ inch diameter. Fruit – none on double-flowering types; summer; 1-3 inches in diameter on single flower types; drupe, indented on one side.
Texture	Medium.
Color	Foliage – shiny green. Flower – pink to rose. Fruit – yellow to pinkish-red.
Culture	Sun. Soil – good drainage; medium fertility. Moisture – medium. Pruning – annually to maintain shape and vigor. Pest Problems – complete spray program annually for control of scale, curculio, peach tree borer, leaf curl, brown rot, and scab. Growth Rate – rapid.
Landscape Notes	Nonfruiting or ornamental flowering peaches widely used for landscape purposes with no regular spray schedule required. Use as screen, border, or specimen where spectacular color display can be appreciated.
Varieties	'Candor' – nonshowy flower; nonbrowning fruit. 'Double White' – double white flowers.

Prunus (proo'nus)
    classical Latin name
    of plum

serrulata (sir-roo-lay'ta)
    having minute, sawlike
    teeth

JAPANESE CHERRY

Family Rosaceae

Zones	6, 7, 8.
Size	Height 15-25 feet; spread 15-20 feet.
Form	Upright with spreading branches. Foliage – alternate, simple, toothed, 2-4 inches long. Flower – April and May; single and double forms, ½-2½ inch diameter. Fruit – summer; ¼ inch diameter; no fruit on double-flowered varieties.
Texture	Medium.
Color	Foliage – medium green; fall, yellowish-orange. Flower – white to pink. Fruit – black.
Culture	Sun to part shade. Soil – very good drainage; medium fertility. Moisture – medium. Pruning – tolerant. Pest Problems – borers, scale, aphids, and various virus dieases. Growth Rate – moderate.
Landscape Notes	Outstanding for quick effect; usual life span 15-20 years. Select fragrant varieties if available.
Varieties	'Jo-nioi' – upright and spreading growth; fragrant single white flowers 1½ inch diameter. 'Kwanzan' – horizontal branching; new foliage copper-red; double pink flowers. Good for street plantings. Very hardy. Correct name is 'Sekiyama.'

Prunus (proo'nus)
  classical Latin
  name of plum

subhirtella (sub-hir-tell'a)
  classical Latin
  name of plum

pendula (pen'dew-la)
  pendulous, hanging

WEEPING CHERRY

Family Rosaceae

Zones	6, 7.
Size	Height 15-20 feet; spread 10-15 feet.
Form	Forked trunk and drooping twiggy branches with slender, whiplike twigs, sometimes shrubby. Foliage – midspring to midfall; alternate, simple, 2-5 inches long. Flower – late March or early April; very numerous in clusters of 2-5, 1 inch wide, single. Fruit – summer; spherical drupes ⅓ inch diameter. Bark – smooth, lustrous, peeling in layers.
Texture	Medium to fine.
Color	Foliage – medium green. Flower – light pink. Fruit – black. Bark – red-brown.
Culture	Sun. Soil – medium drainage; medium fertility. Moisture – medium. Pruning – lightly for shape. Pest Problems – rot, borers, scale, and other insects. Growth Rate – moderate to rapid.
Landscape Notes	Valued for exquisite flowering effect. Graceful and airy. Excellent accent tree. Easily transplanted when young. Grafted on seedling stock of upright species. Not well adapted to Coastal Plains.

Prunus (proo'nus)
  classical Latin name
  of plum

yedoensis (yed-o-en'sis)
  from district of Yeddo
  or Tokyo in Japan

YOSHINO CHERRY

Family Rosaceae

Zones	6, 7.
Size	Height 20-40 feet; spread 20-30 feet.
Form	Upright or pyramidal when young; broad, rounded, or flat-topped with age. Dense with foliage. Foliage – alternate, simple, toothed, 3-5 inches long. Flower – mid-March; single, 1-1½ inches diameter, slightly fragrant. Fruit – summer; ½ inch diameter.
Texture	Medium.
Color	Foliage – pale green; deep brownish-red when unfolding. Flower – white to pink. Fruit – purplish-black.
Culture	Sun. Soil – tolerant. Moisture – medium. Pruning – remove diseased wood and suckers from trunk. Pest Problems – borers. Growth Rate – rapid.
Landscape Notes	Excellent floral display in front of dense evergreens; flowers appear before leaves. Predominant species around Tidal Basin in Washington, D.C. Life span 15-20 years.
Varieties	'Akebono' – softer pink flowers than those of species. Listed in nurseries under synonym 'Daybreak.' 'Perpendens' – irregularly pendulous branches.

Punica (pew'nik-a)
  pomegranate

granatum (gra-na'tum)
  old substantive name

POMEGRANATE

Family Punicaceae

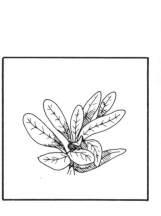

Zones	7,8.
Size	Height 12-15 feet; spread 12-15 feet.
Form	Wide spreading, shrublike. Foliage – opposite, 1½-3 inches long. Flower – May to June: 5-7 wrinkled petals 1-2 inches wide in small clusters, single or double. Fruit – fall: berry 3-5 inch diameter, edible, tart.
Texture	Medium.
Color	Foliage – lustrous green to gray-green. Flower – scarlet-orange, white, yellow, and variegated. Fruit – yellow to red.
Culture	Sun. Soil – tolerant; good drainage; low to medium fertility. Moisture – medium. Pruning – for tree form remove water sprouts annually; thin out excessive growth. Pest Problems – none. Growth Rate – slow.
Landscape Notes	Use as specimen or as high hedge closely planted and pruned. Double-flowering varieties non-fruiting.
Variety	*nana* – dwarf form, 3 feet with scarlet-orange flowers and small decorative fruit. May be used as unclipped hedge.

Pyrus (py'rus)
classical Latin
name of pear tree

calleryana (kall-er-a'na)
named for J.M.M. Callery

CALLERY PEAR

Family Rosaceae

Zones	6, 7, 8.
Size	Height 20-40 feet; spread 20-30 feet.
Form	Upright, semiconical with vertical branching. Medium density. Foliage – alternate, simple, serrated, 2-3½ inches long. Flower – early April; 1 inch diameter in clusters. Fruit – May to June; ½ inch diameter.
Texture	Medium.
Color	Foliage – glossy green; fall, red. Flower – white. Fruit – orange-brown.
Culture	Sun or part shade. Soil – medium to good drainage; medium to low fertility. Moisture – medium. Pruning – lightly for strength and shape. Pest Problems – scale, fruit worms, cedar apple rust, scab, and fire blight. Growth Rate – rapid.
Landscape Notes	Showy display of flowers in early spring; fruit adds interest without creating litter. Beautiful fall foliage color. Useful in formal design. Long lived.
Variety	'Bradford' – vigorous habit of growth; blossoms very cold hardy. Excellent as specimen, screen, or street tree.

Salix (say'licks)
   classical Latin
   for willow

caprea (kap'ree-a)
   pertaining to
   goat

PUSSY WILLOW

Family Salicaceae

Zones	6, 7, 8.
Size	Height 12-25 feet; spread 8-15 feet.
Form	Upright and shrubby with several trunks. Foliage – alternate, simple, toothed, 3-4 inches long. Flower – early spring; showy catkins about 1-1½ inches long. Fruit – capsule.
Texture	Medium.
Color	Foliage – gray-green. Flower – silvery gray. Fruit – brown. Twigs – lustrous brown.
Culture	Sun or part shade. Soil – medium drainage; medium to high fertility. Moisture – medium to high. Pruning – heavy thinning for renovation every 3-5 years. Pest Problems – leaf defoliators, scale, and rusts. Growth Rate – rapid.
Landscape Notes	Used in landscaping as fast growing material. Interesting flowers and fruit for floral arrangements. Short lived.

Sassafras (sas'a-fras)
Spanish salsafras or
Saxifraga supposed to
have similar medicinal
properties

albidum (al'bee-dum)
white

COMMON SASSAFRAS

Family Lauraceae

Zones	6, 7, 8.
Size	Height 25-40 feet; spread 20-25 feet.
Form	Relatively small with numerous crooked branches forming horizontal branching outline. Foliage – late spring to early fall; alternate, simple, 3-5 inches long, 1-3 lobed or entire. Flower – spring; inconspicuous fragrant racemes. Fruit – late summer; drupes on female plants. Bark – aromatic, thick, rough, and fissured on old trunks, with firm, flat ridges.
Texture	Coarse in youth, medium with age.
Color	Foliage – bluish-green; fall, orange to red. Flower – light yellow. Fruit – dark blue with red stalks. Bark – red-brown.
Culture	Sun or part shade. Soil – very tolerant; good drainage; medium fertility in light soil. Moisture – medium. Pruning – remove dead wood and control suckers. Pest Problems – borers and Japanese beetles. Growth Rate – slow.
Landscape Notes	Valuable for gorgeous fall color and fragrant spring bloom. Useful for thickets, borders of woodland parks, and mass plantings. Excellent small tree for landscape use. Horizontal branching habit lends interest; excellent specimen. Difficult to transplant.

Sorbus (sor'bus)
  ancient Latin name

aucuparia (aw-kew-pay'ri-a)
  specific name implying
  bird-catching, from use
  of fruits for this purpose

MOUNTAIN-ASH

Family Rosaceae

Zones	6, 7.
Size	Height 25-30 feet; spread 20-25 feet.
Form	Slender trunk with spreading branches curving up, forming ovate head, fairly dense. Foliage – spring to early fall, alternate, pinnately compound, 9-15 leaflets, each 1-2 inches long. Flower – late spring, after leaves; flat-topped corymbs 4-6 inches wide. Fruit – late summer, persisting; showy clusters of ½ inch wide berries. Bark – smooth and lustrous, becoming rough at base on old trees.
Texture	Fine.
Color	Foliage – light green; fall, reddish. Flower – white. Fruit – orange to red. Bark – gray-green to red-brown.
Culture	Sun. Soil – very tolerant; medium drainage; medium fertility. Moisture – medium. Pruning – remove weak branches. Pest Problems – borers. Growth Rate – rapid.
Landscape Notes	Interesting specimen, showy with fruit, valuable for rocky hills, lawns, and parks. Good small tree for mountains. Easy to transplant. Somewhat short lived.

LARGE TREES — EVERGREEN

Cedrus (see'drus)
old Greek name
for resinous tree

deodara (dee-o-dar'ra)
native name in India
for deodar

DEODAR CEDAR

Family Pinaceae

Zones	6, 7, 8.
Size	Height 40-50 feet; spread 30-40 feet.
Form	Pyramidal with pendulous branches. Foliage – needles 1-2 inches long borne in dense bunches. Fruit – 4 inch long upright cones, rarely produced.
Texture	Fine.
Color	Foliage – bluish-green. Fruit – green.
Culture	Sun or part shade. Soil – medium drainage; medium fertility. Moisture – medium. Pruning – none. Pest Problems – borers may destroy central leader. Growth Rate – rapid.
Landscape Notes	Seedlings vary considerably in foliage color. Should be planted where lower limbs may touch ground. Use as specimen or screen in large-scale areas.

Magnolia (mag-no'li-a)
   named for Pierre Magnol

grandiflora (gran-di-flo'ra)
   large or showy flowered

SOUTHERN MAGNOLIA

Family Magnoliaceae

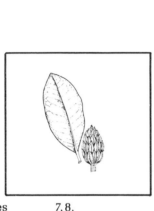

Zones	7, 8.
Size	Height 40-60 feet; spread 25-30 feet.
Form	Conical and symmetrical; medium density. Foliage – alternate, 5-8 inches long. Flower – May to June; 4-6 inch diameter, fragrant. Fruit – late summer and fall; 3-4 inches long, conelike, splitting to disclose seeds.
Texture	Coarse.
Color	Foliage – lustrous dark green. Flower – white. Fruit – gray-brown with red seeds.
Culture	Sun or part shade. Soil – good drainage; medium fertility with high organic content. Moisture – high. Pruning – train young trees for shape. Pest Problems – occasional leaf spot and sun scald. Growth Rate – moderate to rapid.
Landscape Notes	Allow branches to touch ground to hide litter of leaves, flowers, and fruit. Needs ample space to develop well. Use as specimen or large screen. Seedlings vary in characteristics. Difficult to transplant when large.
Varieties	'St. Mary' – dark green leaves; blooms when young. 'Samuel Sommer' – rapid grower; flower 10-14 inch diameter.

Pinus (py'nus)
old Latin name
for pine

palustris (pa-lus'tris)
marsh-loving

LONGLEAF PINE

Family Pinaceae

Zones	7, 8.
Size	Height 80-100 feet; spread 30-40 feet.
Form	Ascending branches and open, rounded head. Foliage – 3 needles in bundle, 10-18 inches long. Fruit – cone 4-6 inches long, stemless.
Texture	Fine.
Color	Foliage – bright green. Fruit – reddish-brown. Buds – white.
Culture	Sun to part shade. Soil – well-drained; medium fertility. Moisture – medium. Pruning – none. Pest Problems – rusts, bark beetles, sawflies, pine-shoot moth, and pine weevils. Growth Rate – rapid.
Landscape Notes	Excellent in mass or as specimen for suburban areas, roadsides or lawns. Of limited use in upper Piedmont and mountains; needles accumulate heavy ice and snow. Difficult to transplant except when young.

Pinus (py'nus)
   old Latin
   name for pine

strobus (stro'bus)
   coned

WHITE PINE

Family Pinaceae

Zones	6, 7.
Size	Height 80-100 feet; spread 30-40 feet.
Form	Symmetrical and pyramidal in youth, becoming irregular with age. Foliage – 3-4 inches long, 5 needles in bundle. Fruit – cone 5-6 inches long, slender and tapering, often curved.
Texture	Fine.
Color	Foliage – gray-green. Fruit – brown. Bark – gray; greenish-gray or tinged red when young.
Culture	Sun. Soil – well-drained; medium fertility. Moisture – medium to high. Pruning – none. Pest Problems – blister rust, weevils, borers, aphids, and woodrot. Growth Rate – rapid in youth.
Landscape Notes	Very handsome when used as ornamental specimen, mass or background; valuable for parks and estates. Good screen until lower branches fall. May be trained as tall hedge. Easy to transplant in large or small sizes. Limited to use in cooler parts of Piedmont and mountains.
Variety	'Pendula' – pendulous branches; fine specimen.

Pinus (py'nus)
old Latin name
for pine

sylvestris (sill-ves'triss)
growing in forests

SCOTCH PINE

Family Pinaceae

Zones	6, 7, 8.
Size	Height 40-70 feet; spread 15-30 feet.
Form	In youth symmetrical pyramid with short, spreading branches; with age very picturesque and open. Foliage – twisted needles 1-3 inches long, 2 in bundle. Fruit – cone 2-3 inches long. Bark – rough, scaling.
Texture	Medium.
Color	Foliage – dark green; winter, bluish-green. Fruit – brown. Bark – red-brown; upper bark bright orange if in favorable environment.
Culture	Sun. Soil – well-drained; medium fertility. Moisture – medium. Pruning – none. Pest Problems – aphids, sawflies, rusts, borers, needle scales, and woodrot. Growth Rate – rapid.
Landscape Notes	Valued for form and character; useful as specimen or in masses. Not suitable for base shrub planting. Easily transplanted.

Pinus (py'nus)
  old Latin name
  for pine

taeda (tae'da)
  cone-bearing, torch-bearing

LOBLOLLY PINE

Family Pinaceae

Zones	6, 7, 8.
Size	Height 70-90 feet; spread 30-40 feet.
Form	Horizontal or ascending branches and rounded head. Foliage – slender, stiff needles 5-10 inches long, 3 in bundle. Fruit – cone 2-5 inches long. Bark – scaly plates; branchlets often glaucous.
Texture	Fine.
Color	Foliage – bright green. Fruit – pale reddish-brown. Bark – red-brown to cinnamon.
Culture	Sun to part shade. Soil – well-drained; medium fertility. Moisture – medium. Pruning – none. Pest Problems – rusts, bark beetles, sawflies, pine-shoot moth, and pine weevils. Growth Rate – rapid.
Landscape Notes	Plant seedlings 12-18 inches in height. Useful in masses as tall windbreak or free-standing as specimen and shade tree. Provides protection for plants requiring light shade. Tolerates poor soil and severe exposures. Difficult to transplant successfully.

Pinus (py'nus)
old Latin name
for pine

thunbergii (thun-ber'gee-eye)
named for
C.P. Thunberg

JAPANESE BLACK PINE

Family Pinaceae

Zones	6, 7, 8.
Size	Height 50-70 feet; spread 25 feet.
Form	Irregular with broad asymmetric head. Branches dense, wide spreading and pendulous. Terminal buds large. Foliage – needles in clusters of 2, 3-5 inches long, stiff and sharply pointed. Fruit – cones 2-3 inches long.
Texture	Medium.
Color	Foliage – dark, bright green. Fruit – brown. Bud – whitish gray.
Culture	Sun. Soil – tolerant. Moisture – low. Pruning – shape. Pest Problems – tip moth and scale larvae of sawfly. Growth Rate – moderate to slow.
Landscape Notes	Best growth in seashore conditions. Useful in rows for bordering drives, property lines, and particularly as screening material spaced 4-6 feet apart. As specimen may be pruned and trained to desired form.

Quercus (kwer'kus)
  classical Latin name
  for oak

laurifolia (lor-ri-fo'li-a)
  with leaves like laurel

LAUREL OAK

Family Fagaceae

Zones	7, 8.
Size	Height 40-60 feet; spread 30-40 feet.
Form	Dense, upright with round top. Foliage – alternate, entire or slightly lobed, semievergreen, 2-5 inches long. Flower – spring; staminate in drooping catkins, pistillate in spikes. Fruit – acorn ⅝ inch long.
Texture	Medium to fine.
Color	Foliage – shining dark green above, light green beneath. Fruit – brown.
Culture	Sun or part shade. Soil – medium drainage; high fertility. Moisture – medium to high. Pruning – none. Pest Problems – none. Growth Rate – slow.
Landscape Notes	Frequently used as street tree. Excellent specimen. Not as strong or long lived as *Q. virginiana*.
Variety	'Darlington' – more compact than species, leaves more persistent.

Quercus (kwer'kus)
    classical Latin
    name for oak

virginiana (vir-gin-i-a'na)
    from Virginia

LIVE OAK

Family Fagaceae

Zones	7,8.
Size	Height 30-50 feet; spread 30-50 feet.
Form	Short trunk; very wide-spreading with horizontal branching. Foliage – alternate, 3-5 inches long, leathery, wavy margin. Flower – hanging catkins. Fruit – acorn 1 inch long.
Texture	Medium.
Color	Foliage – dark green; new growth, bright olive-green. Fruit – dark brown.
Culture	Sun or part shade. Soil – good drainage; medium fertility with high organic content. Moisture – medium. Pruning – none. Pest Problems – none. Growth Rate – slow.
Landscape Notes	May be trained to multiple trunk growth. Magnificent and long-lived specimen for spacious areas in Coastal Plain and Piedmont. Difficult to transplant in large sizes. Needs protection from salt spray. Naturally pruned to large shrub size by sea winds.

Tsuga (soo'ga)
   Japanese name
   for one of
   Asiatic hemlocks

canadensis (kan-a-den'sis)
   from Canada

CANADIAN HEMLOCK

Family Pinaceae

Zones	6, 7.
Size	Height 30-80 feet; spread 15-30 feet.
Form	Slender horizontal branches forming graceful pyramid. Foliage – flat needles ½ inch long. Fruit – cone ½ inch long. Bark – scaly and deeply furrowed.
Texture	Fine.
Color	Foliage – dark green; spring, yellow-green. Fruit – brown. Bark – cinnamon-red to gray.
Culture	Shade or part shade. Soil – good drainage; medium fertility; prefers acid soil. Moisture – medium to high. Pruning – very tolerant. Pest Problems – heart-rot. Growth Rate – rapid.
Landscape Notes	Useful in cool shade and on north slopes in moist soil. Adaptable to formal shearing for high or low hedges or occasional pruning to reduce size. Excellent as screen, border, or large specimen.
Varieties	'Dawsoniana' – slow-growing and compact, to 6 feet in height. *globosa* – dense and rounded form, to 6 feet in height. 'Pendula' – Sargent Hemlock. Broad and moundlike with slightly pendulous branches. Height 6 feet; 10-12 feet wide.

Tsuga (soo'ga)
   Japanese name
   for one of
   Asiatic hemlocks

caroliniana (ka-ro-lin-i-a'na)
   from Carolinas

CAROLINA HEMLOCK

Family Pinaceae

Zones	6, 7.
Size	Height 30-70 feet; spread 20-25 feet.
Form	Compact and pyramidal with rather pendulous branches. Foliage – needles ¾ inch long, encircling twig. Fruit – cone 1½ inches long. Bark – furrowed and scaly.
Texture	Fine.
Color	Foliage – lustrous dark green; new growth, yellow-green. Fruit – brown. Bark – reddish-brown, becoming dull-brown, tinged orange.
Culture	Part shade. Soil – good drainage; high fertility. Moisture – medium to high. Pruning – tolerant. Pest Problems – heart-rot. Growth Rate – rapid.
Landscape Notes	Adapts to city conditions; excellent in cool shaded areas as screen, hedge, and specimen. Limited to use in mountains and Piedmont areas.

LARGE TREES — DECIDUOUS

Acer (a'sir)
   ancient Latin
   name of maple

platanoides (pla-ta-noy'deez)
   like plane tree

NORWAY MAPLE

Family Aceraceae

Zones	6, 7, 8.
Size	Height 60-80 feet; spread 50-70 feet.
Form	Dense and very broad-spreading, regular in outline; in youth almost globose. Foliage – opposite, simple, lobed, 4-7 inches wide. Flower – late March before leaves appear; flat-topped clusters. Fruit — samara, paired.
Texture	Coarse.
Color	Foliage – deep green; fall, yellow. Flower – greenish-yellow. Fruit – brown. Bark – brownish-black.
Culture	Sun. Soil – good drainage; high fertility. Moisture – high. Pruning – none. Pest Problems – none. Growth Rate – moderate.
Landscape Notes	Low-branched, casts dense shade; effect heavier than native maples, stands city conditions better. Useful at seacoast. Easily transplanted. Difficult to establish lawn beneath.
Varieties	'Crimson King' – reddish-purple foliage. 'Globosum' – low growing rounded form; useful for street plantings.

Acer (a'sir)
  ancient Latin
  name of maple

rubrum (roo'brum)
  red

RED MAPLE

Family Aceraceae

Zones	6, 7, 8.
Size	Height 40-50 feet; spread 25-35 feet.
Form	Spreading and symmetrical with ovate or narrow head and ascending branches. Head more irregular than *A. platanoides*. Foliage – opposite, simple, 3-5 lobed, irregularly toothed, 2-4 inches long. Flower – February and March; small but profuse. Fruit – samara, paired, ¾ inch long.
Texture	Medium.
Color	Foliage – medium green, pale green beneath with red petioles; fall, brilliant red or yellow. Flower – red. Fruit – red. Bark – light gray.
Culture	Sun or shade. Soil – medium drainage; medium fertility. Moisture – medium to high. Pruning – shape. Pest Problems – maple insects and diseases. Growth Rate – rapid but does not become brittle.
Landscape Notes	Valuable shade tree of excellent habit and beautiful color sequence; superior to other soft maples. Plant in groups for best effect. Easily transplanted. Long lived.
Variety	'Columnare' – densely upright in habit.

Acer (a'sir)
   ancient Latin
   name of maple

saccharinum (sack-a-ry'num)
   saccharine

SILVER MAPLE

Family Aceraceae

Zones	6, 7, 8.
Size	Height 60-80 feet; spread 50-75 feet.
Form	Short trunk, upright, and fairly open. Foliage – opposite, simple, deeply 5-lobed, 3-6 inches wide. Flower – before leaves appear; inconspicuous. Fruit – samara, 2 inches wide.
Texture	Medium.
Color	Foliage – medium green, silvery beneath; fall, pale yellow. Flower – greenish-yellow. Fruit – greenish-yellow. Bark – silver and gray.
Culture	Sun. Soil – medium drainage; medium to high fertility. Moisture – medium to high. Pruning – during dormant season for growth correction, removal of dead or damaged wood and interfering branches. Pest Problems – leaf gall. Growth Rate – rapid.
Landscape Notes	Soft wood which breaks easily; roots compete with other plantings including lawns. For temporary use only in landscaping. Occasionally useful in parks or estates near water. Easily transplanted.

Acer (a'sir)
    ancient Latin name
    of maple

saccharum (sack-kar'rum)
    old Greek word for sugar

SUGAR MAPLE

Family Aceraceae

Zones	6, 7.
Size	Height 50-75 feet; spread 30-40 feet.
Form	Conical to round top; very dense. Foliage – opposite, simple, 5 lobed, 3-6 inches wide. Flower – inconspicuous. Fruit – samara, paired.
Texture	Medium to coarse.
Color	Foliage – dark green; fall, yellow to orange-red. Flower – yellow. Fruit – greenish-yellow. Bark – dark gray-brown.
Culture	Sun or part shade. Soil – good drainage; medium to high fertility. Moisture – medium. Pruning – none. Pest Problems – anthracnose, leaf spot, leaf blister, and scales. Growth Rate – slow.
Landscape Notes	Gorgeous fall coloring. Young trees susceptible to sun scald if not protected. Grows best in association with other trees and in clean atmosphere. Not suited to Coastal Plain.
Variety	'Temple's Upright' – columnar form.

Carya (ka'ri-a)
    Greek for walnut

illinioensis (ill-i-ni-o-en'sis)
    of Illinois

PECAN

Family Juglandaceae

Zones	6, 7, 8.
Size	Height 60-100 feet; spread 30-40 feet.
Form	Irregular and open with medium density. Foliage – alternate, compound, 12-20 inches long with 11-17 leaflets. Flower – inconspicuous. Fruit – fall; nut enclosed in 4-winged husk.
Texture	Medium.
Color	Foliage – medium green, lighter beneath. Fruit – dark brown.
Culture	Sun or part shade. Soil – medium to good drainage; medium to high fertility. Moisture – high. Pruning – train young trees for strength of branches. Pest Problems – pecan aphid, weevil, scab disease, and leaf defoliators. Growth Rate – moderate.
Landscape . Notes	Unprotected young trees highly susceptible to sun scald. Used as shade tree in parks and estates. Not recommended for residential landscaping since green nuts fall all summer, littering lawns and patios. Brittle. No fall color. Difficult to transplant large sizes.

Catalpa (ka-tal'pa)
North American Indian
name for these trees

bignonioides (big-known-i-oy'deez)
resembling cross vine

SOUTHERN CATALPA

Family Bignoniaceae

Zones	6, 7, 8.
Size	Height 30-50 feet; spread 20-30 feet.
Form	Short, thick trunk and long crooked branches, coarse branchlets and twigs, forming loose, open, irregular head. Foliage – opposite or in 3's, heart-shaped, to 4 inches long. Flower – May; panicles 7 inches long. Fruit – summer; 15 inch pods with beanlike seeds.
Texture	Coarse.
Color	Foliage – dull green. Flower – white. Fruit – green turning brown. Bark – light brown.
Culture	Sun. Soil – good drainage; high fertility. Moisture – high. Pruning – tolerance limited; remove dead and broken branches and maintain shape. Pest Problems – sphinx moth larvae. Growth Rate – rapid.
Landscape Notes	Loose, coarse, untidy tree with handsome flowers and interesting winter effect; useful in parks and large areas. Good as large specimen and for exotic effects. Transplants best when young. Strong, long lived.

Diospyros (dy'os-py-ros)
   Greek grain of Jove,
      referring to edible fruit

virginiana (vir-gin-i-a'na)
   from Virginia

PERSIMMON

Family Ebenaceae

Zones	6,7,8.
Size	Height 40-50 feet; spread 25-30 feet.
Form	Slender, very open and irregular; more symmetrical in open than when mingled with other trees. Foliage – late spring to early fall; alternate, simple, entire, 4-6 inches long. Flower – late spring; small, bellshaped, inconspicuous. Fruit – autumn; pulpy, round berry, 1½ inch diameter; very astringent until frost occurs, then sweet. Bark – deeply cut into rectangles.
Texture	Coarse.
Color	Foliage – deep green; fall, orange. Flower – yellow. Fruit – yellow to orange, marked with purple.
Culture	Sun. Soil – good drainage; high fertility. Moisture – medium to high. Pruning – none. Pest Problems – none. Growth Rate – slow.
Landscape Notes	Grown for fruit and interesting foliage; rather picturesque; landscape value limited. Withstands city conditions. Useful for natural areas, large parks, and roadsides. Difficult to transplant. Fruit attracts wildlife.

Fagus (fay'gus)
    classical Latin
    for birch

grandifolia (gran-di-fo'lee-a)
    large-leaved

BEECH

Family Fagaceae

Zones	6, 7, 8.
Size	Height 60-80 feet; spread 40-60 feet.
Form	Dense and very low-branching with broad rounded crown. Foliage – late spring to very late fall; alternate, simple, sharply toothed, conspicuous parallel veins, 2-5 inches long. Flower – late spring after leaves appear; inconspicuous. Fruit – autumn; triangular nuts in prickly burr. Buds – ¾ inch long, very sharply pointed and slender with many scales.
Texture	Medium.
Color	Foliage – bright green; fall, golden-brown. Bark – light gray, smooth. Bud – brown.
Culture	Sun. Soil – medium drainage; high fertility. Moisture – high. Pruning – tolerant. Pest Problems – bark aphid. Growth Rate – slow.
Landscape Notes	Magnificent specimen casting dense shade which does not permit undergrowth. Excellent for background and framing. Leaves frequently hang on all winter, giving added interest, particularly against dark background. Most suitable for parks and public areas where strong, long lived trees are needed. Difficult to transplant.

Fraxinus (frax'i-nus)
   classical Latin
   for ash

americana (a-me-ri-cay'na)
   from North or South
   America

WHITE ASH

Family Oleaceae

Zones	6, 7.
Size	Height 60-80 feet; spread 50-70 feet.
Form	Broad, rounded head and stout, ascending branches, often broken and ragged from lightning. Foliage – late spring to early fall; opposite, 5-9 leaflets, pinnately compound, 8-12 inches long. Flower – midspring; inconspicuous. Fruit – late summer, often persistent; samara. Bud – broader than long, blunt.
Texture	Medium.
Color	Foliage – bright green; fall, yellow to purple. Bark – deep gray. Bud – brown.
Culture	Sun. Soil – medium drainage; medium to high fertility. Moisture – high. Pruning – tolerant. Pest Problems – scale and stem borer if transplanted from wild. Growth Rate – rapid while young, moderate later.
Landscape Notes	Resists heat and drought well but effectiveness often spoiled by storms and scale. Good park tree for mass planting. May reseed sufficiently to become nuisance. Survives well in severe exposures. Easily transplanted.

Ginkgo (gink'o)
Chinese name for
this tree

biloba (by-low'ba)
two-lobed

MAIDENHAIR TREE

Family Ginkgoaceae

Zones	6, 7, 8.
Size	Height 40-70 feet; spread 20-40 feet.
Form	In youth slender, pyramidal and rather spiky; with age broad and more regular in outline. Foliage – late spring to midfall; alternate, sometimes clustered, 2-lobed, margin wavy or entire, fan-shaped, 2-3½ inches wide. Flower – late spring with leaves; inconspicuous. Fruit – autumn; plumlike, 1 inch diameter. Bark – smooth.
Texture	Medium.
Color	Foliage – bright green; fall, bright yellow. Flower – yellow. Fruit – orange-yellow.
Culture	Sun. Soil – very tolerant; medium drainage; medium fertility. Moisture – medium. Pruning – none. Pest Problems – none. Growth Rate – slow.
Landscape Notes	Exceptional vitality and handsome foliage; very susceptible to air-pollution, otherwise excellent as street tree or specimen for large areas. Casts light shade; sheds leaves rapidly in fall. Avoid planting female tree which produces foul-smelling fruit. May require 20 years to attain mature form. Transplants easily.
Variety	*fastigiata* – columnar habit of growth; useful for narrow spaces.

Gleditsia (gle-dit'si-a)
   named for
   Johann G. Gleditsch,
   director of botanic
   garden at Berlin

triacanthos (try-a-kan'thoss)
   with 3 spines

HONEYLOCUST

Family Fabaceae

Zones	6, 7, 8.
Size	Height 50-75 feet; spread 25-40 feet.
Form	Upright, semiconical, open with age; medium to open density. Foliage – alternate, may be clustered, singly or doubly pinnately compound, 7-12 inches long, leaflets ⅓-1½ inches long. Flower – inconspicuous. Fruit – fall, persistent; 12-18 inch long twisted pod. Twigs – with thorns 4 inches long, typically branched.
Texture	Fine.
Color	Foliage – medium green; fall, yellow. Fruit – brown.
Culture	Sun. Soil – medium to good drainage; medium fertility. Moisture – medium to low. Pruning – train young trees for strength of branches; avoid large pruning wounds. Pest Problems – locust borer, podgall, and webworms. Growth Rate – moderate.
Landscape Notes	Withstands city conditions but thorns present serious hazard on streets and playgrounds. Select thornless and fruitless varieties for landscape use. Easily transplanted.
Variety	'Inermis' – thornless; casts very light shade and endures poor soils.

Liquidambar (liquid-am'bar)
from Latin for liquid
and Arabic for amber, in
allusion to fragrant
resin of Asiatic species

styraciflua (sty-ra-see-flew'a)
sweet-gum-flowing

SWEET-GUM

Family Hamamelidaceae

Zones	6, 7, 8.
Size	Height 60-100 feet; spread 50-75 feet.
Form	Upright and semiconical. Foliage – alternate, simple, 5-7 lobed, star-shaped, 5-7 inches long. Flower – inconspicuous. Fruit – fall; 1 inch diameter, round and prickly. Twigs – frequently winged with cork.
Texture	Medium.
Color	Foliage – dark green; fall, brilliant scarlet or purple. Fruit – brown.
Culture	Sun or part shade. Soil – medium to good drainage; medium to high fertility. Moisture – medium to high. Pruning – train young trees to central trunk. Pest Problems – none. Growth Rate – slow to moderate.
Landscape Notes	Good specimen and attractive all year. Allow sufficient space to develop symmetrically. Most useful for shade, framing, or background in large open areas in parks and along highways. Fruit causes litter in fall and winter. Difficult to transplant in large sizes.

Liriodendron (lir-i-o-den'dron)
   Greek for lily and tree, in
   allusion to shape of
   flowers

tulipifera (too-lip-iff'er-a)
   bearing tuliplike flowers

TULIP-TREE

Family Magnoliaceae

Zones	6, 7, 8.
Size	Height 60-150 feet; spread 30-40 feet.
Form	Very tall and erect with giant columnar trunk and cylindrical head; high branching and spreading with age. Foliage – mid-spring to mid-fall; alternate, simple, lobed, 3-5½ inches long. Flower – mid-April after leaves appear; tuliplike. Fruit – mid-summer, persisting; cone-shaped aggregate of samaras.
Texture	Coarse to medium.
Color	Foliage – light green; fall, bright yellow. Flower – greenish-yellow with orange centers. Fruit – tan.
Culture	Sun. Soil – good drainage; medium fertility. Moisture – medium. Pruning – not tolerant. Pest Problems – aphids. Growth Rate – moderate to rapid.
Landscape Notes	Handsome, stately tree valued for flowers and foliage; useful as specimen or for mass planting in very large areas. Good fall color. Partial leaf drop during dry periods. Difficult to transplant, should be moved when young and in active growth.
Variety	'Fastigiatum' – upright pyramidal form.

Nyssa (nis'sa)
    water nymph, referring
    to habitat of
    native species in
    swampy places

sylvatica (sil-vat'i-ka)
    forest-loving

BLACK TUPELO

Family Nyssaceae

Zones	6, 7, 8.
Size	Height 40-60 feet; spread 20-30 feet.
Form	Tall and narrow with picturesque crown when young; open and irregular in outline with branches spreading horizontally. Foliage – alternate, entire, 2-4 inches long. Flower – midspring; inconspicuous. Fruit – midsummer; berrylike, ½ inch long.
Texture	Medium.
Color	Foliage – lustrous green; fall, brilliant red. Flower – greenish. Fruit – dark blue.
Culture	Sun or shade. Soil – tolerant; medium drainage; medium fertility. Moisture – high. Pruning – tolerance limited. Pest Problems – none. Growth Rate – moderate.
Landscape Notes	Gorgeous fall color and distinctive winter habit; valued for foliage and form. Useful in mass or woodland; good specimen while young. Long lived. Difficult to transplant.

Paulownia (paul-o′ni-a)
    named for Princess
    Anna Paulowna
    of Netherlands

tomentosa (toe-men-toe′sa)
    densely covered with
    matted, flat hairs

EMPRESS-TREE

Family Scrophulariaceae

Zones	6, 7, 8.
Size	Height 30-50 feet; spread 20-30 feet.
Form	Low and spreading branches forming broadly oval and rather open crown. Foliage – opposite, simple, entire or shallowly lobed, to 2 feet wide, pubescent. Flower – midspring before leaves appear; conspicuous 1 foot clusters. Fruit – fall, persisting all winter; ovoid capsule 1½ inches long.
Texture	Very coarse.
Color	Foliage – dark green. Flower – lavender. Fruit – brown.
Culture	Sun. Soil – tolerant; medium drainage; medium fertility. Moisture – medium. Pruning – remove dead wood. Pest Problems – none. Growth Rate – moderate to rapid.
Landscape Notes	Strikingly handsome when in bloom; flower color unusual for trees. Brittle wood but useful as specimen for bold effects in lawns and parks. Transplants best while young.

Platanus (pla'ta-nus)
   classical Greek name
   for plane tree

acerifolia (a-sir-ee-fo'lcc-a)
   maple-leaved

LONDON PLANE-TREE

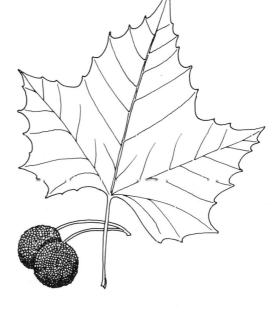

Family Platanaceae

Zones	6, 7, 8.
Size	Height 70-100 feet; spread 50-70 feet.
Form	Medium or short trunk with crown of far-reaching branches; pendulous lower branches; rounded with age. Foliage – late spring to midfall; alternate, simple, lobes to ⅓ depth of blade, 5-10 inches wide. Flower – late spring with leaves; inconspicuous. Fruit – fall; globular heads 1½ inch diameter, 2, 3, or 6 together. Bark – upper very smooth; lower flaking off in large patches.
Texture	Coarse.
Color	Foliage – yellow-green; fall, tan. Fruit – rusty brown. Bark – outer, greenish-gray; inner, white.
Culture	Sun or part shade. Soil – medium drainage; high fertility. Moisture – high. Pruning – remove dead and broken wood. Pest Problems – fungi, borers, and lacebug. Growth Rate – rapid.
Landscape Notes	Very long lived; withstands worst city conditions. Valuable for streets and parks. Requires occasional cleanup of leaves, fruit, and bark. Easily transplanted. Hybrid of *P. occidentalis* x *P. orientalis*.

Platanus (pla'ta-nus)
    classical Greek name
    for plane tree

occidentalis (ok-si-den-tay'lis)
    western, from
    American continent

SYCAMORE

Family Platanaceae

Zones	6, 7, 8.
Size	Height 70-100 feet; spread 60-80 feet.
Form	Very tall and broad with open growth. Often forked into several large secondary trunks with massive, spreading limbs. Foliage – late spring to midfall; alternate, simple, 3-5 shallow lobes, 5-9 inches wide, downy beneath. Flower – inconspicuous. Fruit – fall; globular heads 1½ inch diameter, 1 or 2 together.
Texture	Coarse.
Color	Foliage – light green. Fruit – rusty brown. Bark – upper, green-gray; inner, white; lower, brown-gray.
Culture	Sun or part shade. Soil – medium drainage; high fertility. Moisture – high. Pruning – remove dead and broken wood. Pest Problems – fungi, especially anthracnose, and leaf blight. Growth Rate – very rapid.
Landscape Notes	Withstands severe conditions and city atmosphere; useful as specimen or for mass planting; needs ample space to develop. Bark peels to expose white beneath. Requires periodic cleanup of leaves, fruit, and bark. Easily transplanted.

Prunus (proo'nus)
  classical Latin name
  of plum

sargentii (sar-jent'ee-eye)
  named for Charles Sprague
  Sargent, first director of
  Arnold Arboretum

SARGENT CHERRY

Family Rosaceae

Zones	6, 7, 8.
Size	Height 40-60 feet; spread 30-40 feet.
Form	Upright, rounded and dense with wide-spreading branches. Foliage – alternate, 1-2 inches long. Flower – early spring; single, profuse, 1½ inches wide. Fruit – summer; ½ inch diameter, inconspicuous.
Texture	Medium.
Color	Foliage – medium green; new leaves red-bronze; fall, vivid orange-red. Flower – bright pink. Fruit – black. Bark – shiny black.
Culture	Sun. Soil – good drainage; medium fertility. Moisture – medium. Pruning – tolerant. Pest Problems – usually none; occasionally borers, scale, and aphids. Growth Rate – moderate.
Landscape Notes	Excellent flowering tree for large estates and parks. Casts dense shade; most effective as specimen. Bark effective in winter.
Varieties	'Columnaris' – columnar form. 'Rancho' – upright form growing to 25 feet; for screening, accent, or street tree.

Quercus (kwer'kus)
    classical Latin name
    for oak

alba (al'ba)
    white

WHITE OAK

Family Fagaceae

Zones	6, 7, 8.
Size	Height 60-100 feet; spread 50-90 feet.
Form	Massive and spreading with thick trunk; upper branches ascending and twisting with age, forming broad head. Foliage – late spring to very late fall, often persisting through winter; alternate, simple, 5-9 rounded lobes, 5-8 inches long. Flower – hanging catkins. Fruit – acorn ¾ inch long.
Texture	Coarse to medium.
Color	Foliage – bluish-green; fall, dark red. Flower – pale yellow. Fruit – brown.
Culture	Sun or part shade. Soil – good drainage; medium fertility. Moisture – high. Pruning – none. Pest Problems – none. Growth Rate – slow.
Landscape Notes	Majestic specimen, splendid for any permanent planting in spacious areas. Slow growing but very long lived. Avoid planting near drive-way or patio. Very difficult to transplant.

Quercus (kwer'kus)
 classical Latin
 name for oak

coccinea (kok-sin'ee-a)
 scarlet

SCARLET OAK

Family Fagaceae

Zones	6, 7, 8.
Size	Height 60-80 feet; spread 40-50 feet.
Form	Symmetrical with rounded crown; branches gradually spreading and curving upward. Foliage – late spring to very late fall; alternate, simple, 5-9 toothed lobes, 4-6 inches long, glabrous and thin. Flower – hanging catkins. Fruit – ovoid acorn ¾ inch long.
Texture	Coarse to medium.
Color	Foliage – deep green; fall, red. Flower – pale yellow. Fruit – brown.
Culture	Sun. Soil – good drainage; medium fertility. Moisture – medium. Pruning – none. Pest Problems – none. Growth Rate – rapid.
Landscape Notes	Excellent foliage, pleasing fall color and rapid growth; excellent for framing, background, shade, and street plantings. Difficult to transplant successfully.

Quercus (kwer'kus)
　　classical Latin name
　　for oak

nigra (ny'gra)
　　black

WATER OAK

Family Fagaceae

Zones	6, 7, 8.
Size	Height 50-75 feet; spread 30-40 feet.
Form	Semiconical to round or irregular top; dense; lower branches pendulous. Foliage – alternate, semievergreen, leaves vary from rounded to 3 lobed, 1½-3 inches long. Flower – hanging catkins. Fruit – acorn ½ inch long.
Texture	Medium.
Color	Foliage – glossy dark green; fall, yellowish. Flower – yellow-green.
Culture	Sun or part shade. Soil – medium to good drainage; medium to high fertility. Moisture – medium to high. Pruning – train young trees for central trunk. Pest Problems – gall insects and scale. Growth Rate – moderate to rapid.
Landscape Notes	Frequently used as specimen, canopy, and background. Hybridizes easily, many leaf variations. drooping branches limit use as shade tree. Easily transplanted.

Quercus (kwer'kus)
    classical Latin
    name for oak

palustris (pa-lus'tris)
    marsh-loving

PIN OAK

Family Fagaceae

Zones	6, 7, 8.
Size	Height 60-80 feet; spread 40-50 feet.
Form	Pyramidal with low branching; dense. Foliage – alternate, 5-9 lobed, 4-5 inches long. Flower – hanging catkins. Fruit – acorn ½ inch long.
Texture	Medium to slightly coarse.
Color	Foliage – medium green; fall, red. Flower – yellow green. Fruit – brown.
Culture	Sun or part shade. Soil – medium to good drainage; medium fertility with high clay content. Moisture – medium. Pruning – train young trees to central trunk; permit low branching to ground. Pest Problems – none. Growth Rate – rapid.
Landscape Notes	Excellent lawn tree for large open areas. Not recommended for street or roadway plantings because lower branches block visibility. Holds leaves through winter. Easily transplanted.

Quercus (kwer'kus)
   classical Latin
   name for oak

phellos (fell'os)
   willow

WILLOW OAK

Family Fagaceae

Zones	6, 7, 8.
Size	Height 60-80 feet; spread 30-40 feet.
Form	Graceful and conical in youth, round-topped with age. Foliage – late spring to late fall; alternate, entire, lance-shaped, 2½-5 inches long. Flower – hanging catkins. Fruit – round acorn ½ inch long.
Texture	Fine.
Color	Foliage – bright green; fall, light yellow. Flower – pale yellow. Fruit – brown.
Culture	Sun. Soil – good drainage; medium fertility. Moisture – high. Pruning – none. Pest Problems – none. Growth Rate – rapid to moderate.
Landscape Notes	Interesting and beautiful, of finer texture than other oaks; useful as specimen, framing, background, and canopy. Allow low-branching where space permits. Excellent shade or street tree. Easily transplanted.

Quercus (kwer'kus)
classical Latin name
for oak

rubra (roo'brah)
red

maxima (macks'i-ma)
large or largest

EASTERN RED OAK

Family Fagaceae

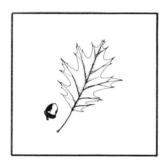

Zones	6, 7, 8.
·Size	Height 50-70 feet; spread 40-60 feet.
Form	Erect and high-branching with several large, spreading branches and slender branchlets; crown pyramidal in youth, round-topped with age. Foliage – late spring to late fall; alternate, simple, 7-11 pointed lobes, 5-9 inches long. Flower – hanging catkins. Fruit – acorn 1 inch long.
Texture	Medium to coarse.
Color	Foliage – deep green; fall, red. Flower – yellow-green. Fruit – brown.
Culture	Sun to part shade. Soil – good drainage; medium fertility. Moisture – medium. Pruning – none. Pest Problems – borers when growth not vigorous. Growth Rate – rapid.
Landscape Notes	Withstands most city conditions. Valued for rapid growth; handsome shade tree for streets, lawns, and mass planting. Transplants more easily than most oaks.

Quercus (kwer'kus)
    classical Latin
    name for oak

velutina (vel-loo'ti-na)
    velvety

BLACK OAK

Family Fagaceae

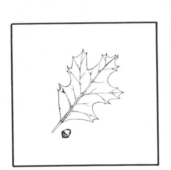

Zones	6, 7, 8.
Size	Height 60-80 feet; spread 30-60 feet.
Form	Wide, irregular, rounded crown; occasionally more narrow with slender branches; sometimes low-branching. Foliage – late spring to late fall, holding dead leaves to midwinter; alternate, usually 7 lobed, base wedge-shaped, to 8 inches long. Flower – hanging catkins. Fruit – acorn ¾ inch long.
Texture	Medium to coarse.
Color	Foliage – lustrous dark green; fall, dull red. Flower – pale yellow. Fruit – brown. Bark – black.
Culture	Sun or part shade. Soil – medium drainage; medium fertility. Moisture – high. Pruning – none. Pest Problems – none. Growth Rate – moderate to slow.
Landscape Notes	One of largest growing oaks; excellent shade tree for parks and woodlands. Tolerates poor soil. Not suitable for small residential lots. Difficult to transplant.

Salix (say'licks)
    classical name
    for willow

babylonica (bab-i-lon'i-ka)
    from ancient Babylon

WEEPING WILLOW

Family Salicaceae

Zones	6, 7, 8.
Size	Height 30-50 feet; spread 20-40 feet.
Form	Slender pendulous branches; fairly compact growth habit. Foliage – alternate, simple, toothed, 5-6 inches long, less than ⅝ inch wide and glabrous. Flower – catkins. Fruit – capsule.
Texture	Fine.
Color	Foliage – medium green. Flower – greenish-yellow. Fruit – brown. Bark – dark brown-black.
Culture	Sun or part shade. Soil – medium drainage; medium to high fertility. Moisture – high. Pruning – head back when young for rigid trunk. Pest Problems – leaf defoliators and cankers. Growth Rate – rapid.
Landscape Notes	Somewhat untidy and aggressive but picturesque when located where billowing form shows to advantage. Use in groups in moist areas as accent or to emphasize rolling terrain. Attractive large screen for areas used in spring and summer; leaves appear in early spring. Should not be planted near underground pipes.

Sophora (soff′or-a)
    from Sophero, Arabic
    name for papilionaceous-
    flowered tree

japonica (ja-pon′i-ka)
    from Japan

JAPANESE PAGODA TREE

Family Fabaceae

Zones	6, 7.
Size	Height 50-70 feet; spread 50 feet.
Form	Wide branching with rounded head. Foliage – alternate, compound with leaflets 2 inches long. Flower – mid-July to September; ⅓ inch long in upright clusters 15 inches long. Fruit – winter; pods 3 inches long.
Texture	Fine.
Color	Foliage – bright green; fall, yellow-brown. Flower – yellowish-white. Fruit – yellow turning brown. Bark – black on trunk; dark green on smaller branches.
Culture	Sun or shade. Soil – very tolerant. Moisture – low. Pruning – tolerant. Pest Problems – none. Growth Rate – moderately rapid.
Landscape Notes	Excellent large street tree or specimen. Use as shade tree for parks and suburban gardens; light foliage permits adequate turf growth.
Varieties	*fastigiata* – upright growth. 'Pendula' – dense, globe-shaped head with pendulous branches. Rarely flowers. *violacea* – leaflets pubescent; flowers with purplish coloration.

Taxodium (tacks-o'di-um)
Greek meaning taxuslike

distichum (dis'ti-kum)
two-ranked, with leaves
or flowers in ranks on
opposite sides of stem

BALD CYPRESS

Family Taxodiaceae

Zones	6, 7, 8.
Size	Height 50-100 feet; spread 20-30 feet.
Form	Pyramidal when young; rounded, spreading, and more open with age. Foliage – needles ½ inch long on lateral branchlets. Fruit – late fall; round cones 1 inch diameter, subdivided into sections.
Texture	Fine.
Color	Foliage – light green; fall, reddish-brown. Fruit – green turning brown.
Culture	Sun or part shade. Soil – medium drainage; medium fertility. Moisture – high to medium. Pruning – none. Pest Problems – none. Growth Rate – slow.
Landscape Notes	Often used as specimen for poorly drained sites but also grows well in average soil. Exotic in appearance. Difficult to transplant.
Variety	'Pendens' – branchlets pendulous.

Tilia (till'i-a)
    old Latin name
    of linden

americana (a-mer-i-cay'na)
    from North or South
    America

AMERICAN LINDEN

Family Tiliaceae

Zones	6, 7, 8.
Size	Height 60-80 feet; spread 50-60 feet.
Form	Tall and stately with rounded head and low wide-spreading branches. Foliage – alternate, simple, toothed, usually heart-shaped, 3-6 inches long. Flower – early summer; drooping cymes, fragrant. Fruit – early fall; nutlike with stalk attached to narrow leafy bract.
Texture	Coarse.
Color	Foliage – bright green; fall, yellow. Flower – ivory or creamy. Fruit – buff or mustard-color.
Culture	Sun or part shade. Soil – good drainage; high fertility. Moisture – medium to high. Pruning – tolerant. Pest Problems – root rot. Growth Rate – rapid.
Landscape Notes	Useful as shade or canopy for parks. Recommended for cooler areas. Easily transplanted while young.
Variety	'Fastigiata' – narrow pyramidal form.

Tilia (till'i-a)
    old Latin name
    of linden

cordata (kor-day'ta)
    heart-shaped

LITTLELEAF LINDEN

Family Tiliaceae

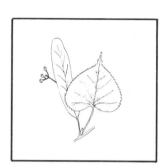

Zones	6, 7, 8.
Size	Height 30-50 feet; spread 25-40 feet.
Form	Pyramidal and dense with ascending, spreading branches. Foliage – midspring to late fall; alternate, simple, toothed, usually broader than long, 1½-3 inches long. Flower – May; fragrant cymes. Fruit – fall, persisting; nutlike with stalk attached to narrow leafy bract.
Texture	Fine to medium.
Color	Foliage – dark green, bluish gray beneath. Flower – creamy yellow.
Culture	Sun or part shade. Soil – good drainage; medium fertility. Moisture – medium to high. Pruning – remove unduly heavy side limbs in youth. Pest Problems – Leopard Moth larvae. Growth Rate – moderate to slow.
Landscape Notes	Valuable for city conditions and poor soil. Useful as street tree and for areas requiring dense shade. More refined than *T. americana*. Useful as lawn tree but casts dense shade which limits turf growth. Easily transplanted.
Varieties	'Greenspire' – straight single trunk; excellent street tree. 'Pyramidalis' – widely pyramidal habit. 'Swedish Upright' narrow and upright with short side branches.

Ulmus (ul'mus)
  classical Latin
  name of elm

americana (a-me-ri-cay'na)
  from North or South
  America

AMERICAN ELM

Family Ulmaceae

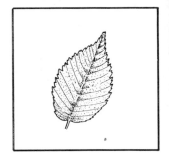

Zones	6, 7, 8.
Size	Height 75-125 feet; spread 60-120 feet.
Form	Irregular, widely arching branches forming vase-shape; angles of branches acute. Foliage – alternate, simple, toothed, 4-6 inches long. Flower – inconspicuous. Fruit – samara ½ inch long.
Texture	Medium to coarse.
Color	Foliage – dark green; fall, yellow. Fruit – green. Bark – dark gray.
Culture	Sun or part shade. Soil – medium drainage; medium fertility. Moisture – medium. Pruning – remove broken or dying branches. Pest Problems – insects, Dutch Elm disease, and mildew. Growth Rate – slow.
Landscape Notes	Beautiful habit of growth; formerly widely planted on boulevards and parkways but susceptibility to Dutch Elm disease now limits landscape use.

Zelkova (zel-ko'va)
    after vernacular name
    Zelkoua in Crete or
    Selkeva in Caucasus

serrata (ser-ra'ta)
    serrate

JAPANESE ZELKOVA

Family Ulmaceae

Zones	6, 7, 8.
Size	Height 50-60 feet; spread 40-50 feet.
Form	Short trunk with ascending branches and round head, graceful. Foliage – alternate, simple, toothed, 2-5 inches long. Flower – inconspicuous. Fruit – pea-size, hard, inconspicuous.
Texture	Medium to fine.
Color	Foliage – deep green; fall, yellow to reddish-brown.
Culture	Sun or part shade. Soil – tolerant. Moisture – medium. Pruning – none. Pest Problems – none. Growth Rate – moderate to rapid.
Landscape Notes	Excellent shade tree. Frequently used as street tree or lawn specimen. Substitute for elm; apparently resistant to Dutch Elm disease. Trunk subject to sun scald.
Variety	'Village Green' – slightly arching branches; similar in form to American Elm.

PLANT LISTS

Plants Requiring Extra Care for Best Appearance

Ground covers
  Dichondra repens carolinensis
  Fragaria chiloensis ananassa

Vines
  Clematis hybrida
  Ficus pumila
  Rosa hybrida
  Smilax lanceolata
  Vitis rotundifolia
  Wisteria floribunda
  Wisteria sinensis

Shrubs 1-4 feet
  Daphne odora
  Euonymus fortunei 'Vegetus'
  Euonymus japonicus 'Microphyllus'

Shrubs 4-6 feet
  Buxus microphylla japonica
  Gardenia jasminoides
  Vaccinium ashei

Shrubs 6-12 feet
  Buddleia davidii
  Euonymus japonicus
  Kolkwitzia amabilis
  Syringa persica
  Syringa vulgaris

Trees
  Malus pumila
  ·Prunus persica

Large Shrubs and Trees for Restricted Root Space
(less than 6 feet wide)

  Koelreuteria paniculata
  Lagerstroemia indica
  Ligustrum japonicum
  Nerium oleander
  Prunus caroliniana
  Prunus cerasifera 'Atropurpurea'

Plants for Beach Places

Full exposure
  Elaeagnus pungens
  Ilex vomitoria
  Myrica pensylvanica
  Parthenocissus quinquefolia
  Quercus virginiana
  Tamarix gallica
  Vitis rotundifolia
  Yucca varieties

Minimum protection
  any above, plus
  Euonymus fortunei varieties
  Euonymus japonicus
  Pittosporum tobira
  Raphiolepis umbellata
  Rosa rugosa
  Sabal palmetto
  Santolina chamaecyparissus

Medium protection
  any above, plus
  Clematis paniculata
  Cleyera japonica
  Cortaderia selloana
  Fatshedera lizei
  Fatsia japonica
  Gelsemium sempervirens
  Hemerocallis hybrida
  Iberis sempervirens
  Ilex opaca
  Juniperus chinensis
  Juniperus chinensis 'Pfitzeriana'
  Juniperus conferta
  Juniperus horizontalis
  Ligustrum japonicum
  Lonicera sempervirens
  Myrica cerifera
  Nerium oleander
  Pinus thunbergii
  Podocarpus macrophyllus maki
  Prunus caroliniana
  Rosa banksiae
  Rosa wichuraiana
  Santolina virens

Thorny Plants for Barrier Hedges

Berberis julianae
Berberis thunbergii
Berberis verruculosa
Chaenomeles japonica
Chaenomeles speciosa
Elaeagnus angustifolia
Elaeagnus pungens
Ilex aquifolium
Ilex cornuta varieties
Ilex opaca
Mahonia aquifolium
Mahonia bealei
Osmanthus heterophyllus
Pyracantha coccinea
Rosa hybrida
Rosa multiflora
Rosa rugosa
Rosa wichuraiana

Plants for Espalier

Camellia japonica
Cercis canadensis
Chaenomeles japonica
Chaenomeles speciosa
Cornus florida
Cornus kousa
Cotoneaster dammeri
Cotoneaster horizontalis
Euonymus alatus
Forsythia intermedia
Ilex cornuta 'Burfordii'
Ilex crenata varieties
Jasminum nudiflorum
Juniperus chinensis 'Pfitzeriana'
Magnolia grandiflora
Magnolia soulangeana
Magnolia stellata
Malus hybrida
Malus pumila
Osmanthus fragrans
Photinia serrulata
Prunus persica
Prunus serrulata
Prunus subhirtella pendula
Pyracantha coccinea
Pyracantha koidzumi
Taxus cuspidata
Viburnum plicatum tomentosum

Shrubs Tolerating Full Shade

Dry Soil
Berberis thunbergii
Hamamelis virginiana
Hypericum calycinum
Ligustrum varieties
Myrica varieties
Raphiolepis umbellata

Wet Soil
Amelanchier canadensis
Azalea (Rhododendron) calendulacea
Azalea (Rhododendron) nudiflora
Ilex cassine
Ilex glabra
Ilex vomitoria
Kalmia latifolia
Leucothoe fontanesiana
Magnolia virginiana
Myrica varieties

Plants for Bank Planting

Akebia quinata
Berberis thunbergii
Celastrus scandens
Clematis paniculata
Cotoneaster horizontalis
Euonymus fortunei 'Coloratus'
Forsythia intermedia
Hedera helix
Hypericum calycinum
Jasminum floridum
Jasminum nudiflorum
Juniperus conferta
Juniperus horizontalis varieties
Leucothoe fontanesiana
Myrica cerifera
Myrica pensylvanica
Parthenocissus quinquefolia
Parthenocissus tricuspidata
Rosa banksiae
Rosa wichuraiana
Rosmarinus officinalis 'Prostratus'
Vinca minor
Vitis rotundifolia

Trees Withstanding City Conditions

Acer platanoides
Albizia julibrissin
Elaeagnus angustifolia
Gleditsia triacanthos 'Inermis'
Koelreuteria paniculata
Lagerstroemia indica
Magnolia grandiflora
Magnolia soulangeana
Magnolia stellata
Malus hybrida varieties

Platanus acerfolia
Platanus occidentalis
Pyrus calleryana
Quercus rubra maxima
Quercus coccinea
Sabal palmetto
Sophora japonica
Tilia cordata
Tsuga caroliniana

Tree Heights at 10 Years

Botanical name	Common name	Height in Feet
Acer platanoides	Norway Maple	16-19
Acer rubrum	Red Maple	20
Acer saccharinum	Silver Maple	26
Acer saccharum	Sugar Maple	22
Fraxinus americana	White Ash	20
Ginkgo biloba	Maidenhair Tree	14-18
Gleditsia triacanthos 'Moraine'	Honey Locust	26
Liquidambar styraciflua	Sweetgum	19
Liriodendron tulipifera	Tulip Tree	17
Magnolia grandiflora	Southern Magnolia	14
Nyssa sylvatica	Black Tupelo	15
Pinus nigra	Austrian Pine	15
Pinus strobus	White Pine	21
Pinus sylvestris	Scotch Pine	20
Pinus thunbergii	Japanese Black Pine	10
Platanus acerfolia	London Plane Tree	29
Platanus occidentalis	Sycamore	34
Quercus alba	White Oak	14
Quercus palustris	Pin Oak	19
Quercus phellos	Willow Oak	21
Quercus rubra maxima	Eastern Red Oak	18
Quercus virginiana	Live Oak	14
Sabal palmetto	Palmetto	20
Salix babylonica	Weeping Willow	21
Taxodium distichum	Bald Cypress	15
Tilia americana	American Linden	20
Tilia cordata	Littleleaf Linden	26
Tsuga canadensis	Canadian Hemlock	15
Ulmus americana	American Elm	30

BIBLIOGRAPHY

Bailey, L. H. 1949. *Manual of Cultivated Plants.* The Macmillan Company. New York, N.Y.

Graetz, Karl E. 1973. *Seacoast Plants of the Carolinas.* U.S. Department of Agriculture, Soil Conservation Service.

Hume, H. Harold. 1953. *Hollies.* The Macmillan Company. New York, N.Y.

Lee, Frederick P. 1965. *The Azalea Book.* D. Van Nostrand Company. Princeton, New Jersey.

Pirone, Pascal P. 1960. *Diseases and Pests of Ornamental Plants.* The Ronald Press Company. New York, N.Y.

Robinson, Florence Bell. 1960. *Useful Trees and Shrubs.* Garrard Publishing Company. Champaign, Illinois.

Taylor, Norman. 1957. *Taylor's Encyclopedia of Gardening.* Houghton Mifflin Company. Boston, Massachusetts.

Taylor, Norman. 1965. *The Guide to Garden Shrubs and Trees.* Houghton Mifflin Company. Boston, Massachusetts.

Thode, Frederick W. 1974. *Woody Plant Material for Landscape Use.* Department of Horticulture, Clemson University, Clemson, South Carolina

Van Veen, Ted. 1969. *Rhododendrons in America.* Sweeney, Krist, and Dimm, Inc. Portland, Oregon.

Wigginton, Brooks E. 1963. *Trees and Shrubs for the Southeast.* University of Georgia Press. Athens, Georgia.

Wyman, Donald. 1965. *Trees for American Gardens.* The Macmillan Company. New York, N.Y.

Wyman, Donald. 1969. *Shrubs and Vines for American Gardens.* The Macmillan Company. New York, N.Y.

Wyman, Donald. 1970. *Ground Cover Plants.* The Macmillan Company. New York, N.Y.

INDEX

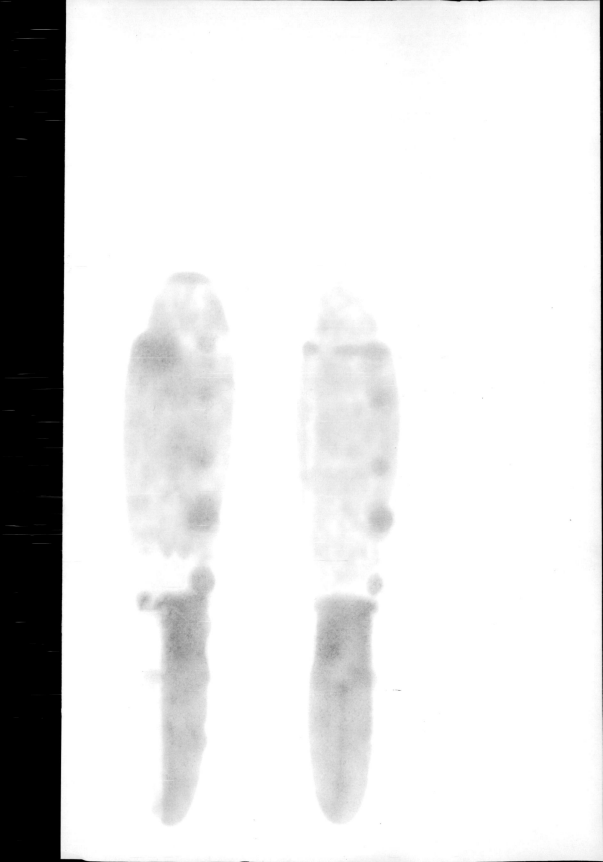